The popular supers
festive amuseme1
Highlanders of Scotland

William Grant Stewart

Alpha Editions

This edition published in 2024

ISBN 9789361473265

Design and Setting By

Alpha Editions

www.alphaedis.com

Email - info@alphaedis.com

Contents

PREFACE.

NO part of the United Kingdom has of late years attracted a greater portion of public attention than the Highlands of Scotland. Formerly isolated as the inhabitants were from their fellow subjects, by a different language and separate interests, their character was but little known and less admired. Devoted to their chiefs and feudal institutions, they entertained a sovereign contempt for their neighbours; and, in their occasional intercourse with them, displayed feelings and manners little calculated to gain confidence or secure esteem.

But when the Rebellion in 1745, and its consequences, nearly annihilated feudal power, and broke down the wall of partition, by which the mountaineer was so long divided from the inhabitant of the plain, a new light was reflected upon his manners and habits. The gradual establishment of commercial and friendly relations with the inhabitants of other countries, accelerated the decay of mutual prejudices; and the virtues of the Highlander, which were previously reserved for home consumption, were now duly appreciated by the world. He no longer appeared the rude and unprincipled depredator, but the generous and disinterested character, whose romantic and chivalrous habits were rendered peculiarly interesting, as the remains of those boldly defined virtues which distinguished our primitive ancestors. Accordingly, the genius of the age became speedily alive to the importance of so novel and interesting a character. Shaping its course to the Highland mountains, it discovered among their unexplored recesses, those plentiful materials, on which are founded some of the most splendid works which adorn the circle of British literature.

Nor have all those superstructures yet exhausted so fertile a mine. Notwithstanding all the research that has been employed in tracing the origin, and delineating the manners of the inhabitants, and the many ingenious descriptions we have had of their local scenery, there are still many hidden treasures left for discovery, which presently languish in obscurity. This observation applies with great truth to those more remote and romantic regions, which, from their secluded situations, had been long inaccessible to the approach of learning and genius; and where the native inhabitants, from want of intercourse with their more refined and effeminate countrymen, are the true representatives of our ancient forefathers in their various feelings and habits.

Of the manners and character of this noble and poetic race of mountaineers, little was known further than what may be collected from the manners of their contemporaries, in more accessible parts of the country. The great defect which especially exists in the delineation of the Highlander's superstitions, becomes peculiarly apparent to one, who had an opportunity of investigating those relics of the less polished ages of the world, as they are still exhibited in the habits of the people of whom we are writing. Many of the more prominent and common features of this branch of our national peculiarities have, indeed, been long ago celebrated by the pens of the immortal Burns, Ramsay, Sir Walter Scott, and others of less note, while much light has been thrown on the general character of the Scottish Highlander, by the ingenious Mrs. Grant of Laggan, and the gallant General Stewart of Garth; but the more interesting and latent peculiarities have been left to expire in the dark. The want of a complete and systematic account of the Highland and Scottish Superstitions, is a desideratum in our national literature, which the philosophic mind will readily regret; and this regret will be the more sincere on reflecting, that, from the fading aspects those interesting relics have now assumed, it is a desideratum which, in the course of a few years, cannot be supplied. The decline of popular romance is keeping pace with the progress of knowledge and civilization,—which, as they illumine the unenlightened mind, open it to the folly of its prejudices; and thus the time is hastening its approach, when the natives of our remotest glens shall be no longer inspired with reverence for the fairy turret, nor shall their social circle be contracted by the frightful tale.

Far be it, however, from the writer of these pages to wish the reign of superstition prolonged. But, while he would hail with delight, the total extirpation of every prejudice tending to enslave the mental energy of the noble Gael, he would as ardently desire their perpetuation on the page of history, as his ancient peculiarities. Divested as they will soon be of their formidable character, we would preserve them as the most ancient relics we could transmit to our posterity, to whom, in the course of a few centuries, they may appear as preposterous and incredible, as the Poems of Ossian do now to the more sceptical part of the present generation.

It was not, however, the writer's conviction of the utility of such a work as this alone, that induced him to undertake a task for which, he is afraid, he will be found to have been ill qualified. A considerable time ago, and at a very early period of life, an impaired state of health rendered it necessary for him to abandon his professional labours for a time, and to retire from the metropolis to the place of his nativity. The lassitude of mind consequent on a total remission from all employment, induced him to seek some rational source of amusement; and the idea of investigating the opinions and customs of his countrymen, was suggested to him by various circumstances, as likely to afford instruction as well as entertainment. His opportunities were most ample, and his task of course, comparatively easy.

Surrounded by the most original, brave, and ingenious class of Highlanders existing, and possessing considerable knowledge of their language and manners, the writer found it no difficult matter to become completely acquainted with their prejudices and habits. By visiting the most celebrated professors of traditional lore in the district, he speedily acquired not only a fundamental knowledge of the reigning principles of superstition but likewise an inexhaustible store of tales and traditions. And by mingling occasionally with the peasantry in their public and private festivities, he was enabled, from personal observation, to draw faithful portraits of those scenes of mirth and festivity, for which the inhabitants are so eminently distinguished. The result of his observations afforded him so much satisfaction that he thought it worth while from time to time, to commit the particulars to paper,—not with the view of urging them on the public, but for his own private amusement. But the increasing avidity with which traits of the Highland Superstitions have been received as developed in the tales of the day, suggested to him the idea of submitting his gleanings to the public, in the form of a detailed account of the Superstitions and Festivities of the Highlanders of Scotland; and he hopes, however defective may be its execution, the design is not altogether unworthy of public patronage.

To arrange his gleanings in a connected and systematic order, was an undertaking far more tedious than the collection of them. The traits of Highland superstition are of so various and heterogeneous a character, that it appeared almost wholly impracticable to connect and digest them into the form of a connected narrative; and yet in any other shape they would necessarily loose much of the interest which they possess in their present form. Sensible of this he has endeavoured to the best of his ability, to arrange the different traits under their proper heads, in the most systematic and connected manner practicable, without introducing extraneous matter, which would not only destroy the native complexion of the subject, but also swell the limits of the work. By excluding solemn dissertation from such ludicrous relations as the following, he has been enabled to compress many particulars into little space, while his delineations possess a greater degree of truth and fidelity. To illustrate the various traits set forth, the writer has interspersed his delineations with a collection of the most popular tales of the day. These tales, whether they be the creation of the imagination, or the offspring of the credulity of their own original authors, cannot now fail to interest the philosopher or the antiquary, while they may amuse the less profound. For, utterly destitute of all probability, and broadly ludicrous as they may appear to the polished reader, they are, nevertheless, those interesting channels, by which the feelings and habits of our earliest forefathers have been kept alive and transmitted down, through so many changeful ages, to their posterity of the present day.

The length of those primitive relations is necessarily much abridged, but a strict regard has been had to their original style and phraseology. The language is almost entirely borrowed from the mouth of the Highland narrator, and translated, it is hoped, in a manner so simple and unvarnished, as to be perfectly intelligible to the capacity of the peasant, for whose fire-side entertainment this little volume may, perhaps, be peculiarly adapted.

PART I.

"The gleaming path of the steel winds through the gloomy ghost. The form fell shapeless into air, like a column of smoke which the staff of the boy disturbs as it rises from the half-extinguished furnace."

OSSIAN.

CHAPTER I.
OF THE HIGHLAND GHOSTS IN GENERAL.

OF whatever country, station, or character the reader may be, we presume it will be unnecessary for us, on this our outset, to intrude upon his time by entering into a logical definition of the term *Ghost*. There is perhaps no nation or clime, from California to Japan, where that very ancient and fantastic race of beings called Ghosts is not, under different terms and different characters, more or less familiar to the inhabitants. We do not mean, however, to follow this fleeting race of patriarchs throughout their wide course of wandering and colonisation from the beginning of time to the present day—as, in all likelihood, our research would turn out equally arduous and unprofitable; we confine our lucubrations to the colony of the tribe which, from time immemorial, have settled themselves among the inhabitants of the Highland Mountains.

Be it known then to the reader, that, so early as the days of Ossian, the son of Fingal, and ever since, ghosts have been at all times a plentiful commodity among the hills of Caledonia. Every native Highlander has allied to him, from his birth, one of those airy beings in the character of an auxiliary or helpmate, who continues his companion, not only during all the days of the Highlander's life, but also for an indefinite period of time after his decease. It will be readily believed that this ancient class of our mountaineers cannot have descended through so many changeful ages of the world without sharing, in some measure, those revolutions of manners and habits to which all classes and communities of people are equally liable. Accordingly the ghost has suffered as great a degeneracy from that majesty of person and chivalry of habits which anciently distinguished the primitive inhabitants of Caledonia, as his mortal contemporary, man. Unlike the present puny, green, worm-eaten effigies that now-a-days stalk about our premises, and, like the cameleon, feed upon the air, the ancient race of Highland ghosts were a set of stout, lusty, sociable ghosts, *"as tall as a pine, and as broad as a house."* Differing widely in his habits from those of his posterity, the ghost of antiquity would enter the habitation of man, descant a lee-long night upon the news of the times, until the long-wished-for supper was once prepared, when this pattern of frankness and good living would invite himself to the table, and do as much justice to a bicker of Highland crowdie as his earthly contemporaries. Indeed, if all tales be true, many centuries are not elapsed since those social practices of the ghosts of the day proved an eminent pest to society. With voracious appetites, those greedy gormandizers were in the habit of visiting the humble hamlets, where superabundance of store seldom resided, and of ravishing from the grasp of a starving progeny the meagre fare allotted to their support.

Beyond their personal attractions, however, it is believed they displayed few enviable qualities; for, besides their continual depredations on the goods and chattels of the adjacent hamlets, they were ill-natured and cruel, and cared not a spittle for woman or child. The truth of this remark is well exemplified in the history of two celebrated ghosts, who *"once upon a time"* lived, or rather existed, in the Wilds of *Craig-Aulnaic*, a romantic place in the district of Strathdown, Banffshire. The one was a male, and the other a female. The male was called *Fhua Mhoir Bein Baynac*, after one of the mountains of Glenavon, where at one time he resided; and the female was called *Clashnichd Aulnaic*, from her having had her abode in *Craig-Aulnaic*. But, although the great ghost of *Ben-Baynac* was bound, by the common ties of nature and of honour, to protect and cherish his weaker companion, *Clashnichd Aulnaic*, yet he often treated her in the most cruel and unfeeling manner. In the dead of night, when the surrounding hamlets were buried in deep repose, and when nothing else disturbed the solemn stillness of the midnight scene, "oft," says our narrator, "would the shrill shrieks of poor *Clashnichd* burst upon the slumberer's ears, and awake him to any thing but pleasant reflections."

But of all those who were incommoded by the noisy and unseemly quarrels of these two ghosts, James *Owre* or Gray, the tenant of the farm of Balbig of Delnabo, was the greatest sufferer. From the proximity of his abode to their haunts, it was the misfortune of himself and family to be the nightly audience of *Clashnichd's* cries and lamentations, which they considered any thing but agreeable entertainment.

One day, as James Gray was on his rounds looking after his sheep, he happened to fall in with *Clashnichd*, the Ghost of Aulnaic, with whom he entered into a long conversation. In the course of this conversation he took occasion to remonstrate with her on the very disagreeable disturbance she caused himself and family, by her wild and unearthly cries,—cries which, he said, few mortals could relish in the dreary hours of midnight. Poor *Clashnichd*, by way of apology for her conduct, gave James Gray a sad account of her usage, detailing at full length the series of cruelties committed upon her by *Ben-Baynac*. From this account, it appeared that her cohabitation with the latter was by no means a matter of choice with *Clashnichd*; on the contrary, it appeared that she had, for a long time, led a life of celibacy with much comfort, residing in a snug dwelling, as already mentioned, in the wilds of Craig-Aulnaic; but *Ben-Baynac* having unfortunately taken it into his head to pay her a visit, he took a fancy, not to herself, but her dwelling, of which, in his own name and authority, he took immediate possession, and soon after expelled poor *Clashnichd*, with many stripes, from her natural inheritance; while, not satisfied with invading and depriving her of her just rights, he was in the habit of following her into her private haunts, not with the view of offering her any endearments, but for the purpose of inflicting on her person every degrading torment which his brain could invent.

Such a moving relation could not fail to affect the generous heart of James Gray, who determined from that moment to risk life and limb in order to vindicate the rights and revenge the wrongs of poor *Clashnichd* the Ghost of Craig-Aulnaic. He therefore took good care to interrogate his new *protegé* touching the nature of her oppressor's constitution, whether he was of that *killable* species of ghost that could be shot with a silver sixpence, or if there was any other weapon that could possibly accomplish his annihilation. *Clashnichd* informed him that she had occasion to know that *Ben-Baynac* was wholly invulnerable to all the weapons of man, with the exception of a large mole on his left breast, which was no doubt penetrable by silver or steel; but that, from the specimens she had of his personal prowess and strength, it were vain for mere man to attempt to combat *Ben-Baynac* the great ghost. Confiding, however, in his expertness as an archer—for he was allowed to be the best marksman of his age—James Gray told *Clashnichd* he did not fear him with all his might,—that *he* was his man; and desired her, moreover, next time he chose to repeat his incivilities to her, to apply to him, James Gray, for redress.

It was not long ere he had an opportunity of fulfilling his promises. *Ben-Baynac* having one night, in the want of better amusement, entertained himself by inflicting an inhuman castigation on *Clashnichd*, she lost no time in waiting on James Gray, with a full and particular account of it. She found him smoking his *cutty*, and unbuttoning his habiliments for bed; but, notwithstanding the inconvenience of the hour, James needed no great persuasion to induce him to proceed directly along with *Clashnichd* to hold a communing with their friend *Ben-Baynac* the great ghost. *Clashnichd* was a stout sturdy hussey, who understood the knack of travelling much better than *our* women do. She expressed a wish that, for the sake of expedition, James Gray would mount himself on her ample shoulders, a motion to which the latter agreed; and a few minutes brought them close to the scene of *Ben-Baynac's* residence. As they approached his haunt, he came forth to meet them, with looks and gestures which did not at all indicate a cordial welcome. It was a fine moonlight night, and they could easily observe his actions. Poor *Clashnichd* was now sorely afraid of the great ghost. Apprehending instant destruction from his fury, she exclaimed to James Gray that they would be both dead people, and that immediately, unless James could hit with an arrow the mole which covered *Ben-Baynac's* heart. This was not so difficult a task as James had hitherto apprehended it. The mole was as large as a common bonnet, and yet nowise disproportioned to the natural size of his body, for he certainly was a great and a mighty ghost. *Ben-Baynac* cried out to James Gray, that he would soon make eagle's-meat of him; and certain it is, such was his intention, had not James Gray so effectually stopped him from the execution of it. Raising his bow to his eye when within a few yards of *Ben-Baynac*, he took an important aim; the arrow flew—it hit—a yell from *Ben-Baynac* announced its fatality. A hideous howl re-echoed from the surrounding mountains, responsive to the groans of a thousand ghosts; and *Ben-Baynac*, like the smoke of a shot, evanished into air.

Clashnichd, the Ghost of Aulnaic, now found herself emancipated from the most abject state of slavery, and restored to freedom and liberty, through the invincible courage of James Gray. Overpowered with gratitude, she fell at James Gray's feet, and vowed to devote the whole of her time and talents towards his service and prosperity. Meanwhile, being anxious to have her remaining goods and furniture removed to her former dwelling, whence she had been so iniquitously expelled by *Ben-Baynac* the great ghost, she requested of her new master the use of his horses to remove them. James observing on the adjacent hill a flock of deer, and wishing to have a trial of his new servant's sagacity or expertness, told her those were his horses,— she was welcome to the use of them; desiring, when she had done with them, that she would inclose them in his stable. *Clashnichd* then proceeded to make use of the horses, and James Gray returned home to enjoy his night's rest.

Scarce had he reached his arm-chair, and reclined his cheek on his hand, to ruminate over the bold adventure of the night, when *Clashnichd* entered, with her "breath in her throat," and venting the bitterest complaints at the unruliness of his horses, which had broken one-half of her furniture, and caused more trouble in the stabling of them than their services were worth. "Oh! they are stabled, then?" inquired James Gray. *Clashnichd* replied in the affirmative. "Very well," rejoined James, "they shall be tame enough to-morrow."

From this specimen of *Clashnichd* the Ghost of Craig-Aulnaic's expertness, it will be seen what a valuable acquisition her service proved to James Gray and his young family; of which, however, they were too speedily deprived by a most unfortunate accident. From the sequel of the story, and of which the foregoing is but an extract, it appears that poor *Clashnichd* was but too deeply addicted to those guzzling propensities which at that time rendered her kin so obnoxious to their human neighbours. She was consequently in the habit of visiting her friends much oftener than she was invited, and, in the course of such visits, was never very scrupulous in making free with any eatables that fell within the circle of her observation.

One day, while engaged on a foraging expedition of this description, she happened to enter the Mill of Delnabo, which was inhabited in those days by the miller's family. She found the miller's wife engaged in roasting a large gridiron of fine savoury fish, the agreeable effluvia proceeding from which perhaps occasioned her visit. With the usual inquiries after the health of the miller and his family, *Clashnichd* proceeded, with the greatest familiarity and good humour, to make herself comfortable at the expense of their entertainment. But the miller's wife, enraged at the loss of her fish, and not relishing such unwelcome familiarity, punished the unfortunate *Clashnichd* rather too severely for her freedom. It happened that there was at the time a large caldron of boiling water suspended over the fire, and this caldron the beldam of a miller's wife overturned in *Clashnichd's* bosom! Scalded beyond recovery, she fled up the wilds of Craig-Aulnaic, uttering the most melancholy lamentations, nor has she been ever since heard of to the present day.

CHAPTER II.
OF THE GHOST IN HIS CO-EXISTENT STATE—HIS PERSONAL SIMILITUDES AND HABITS.

HAVING, in the preceding chapter, endeavoured, as briefly as possible, to throw some light upon the general character of the primitive race of Highland ghosts in order to enable the reader to judge of the difference of manners which distinguished them from the modern ghosts, we shall now proceed to the consideration of the latter during the interval betwixt the birth and the eve of the death of the mortal, and which, for the sake of illustration, we shall call his co-existent state.

From the birth of the mortal to the eve of his death, the ghost, in point of similitude, is a perfect counterpart or representative of his earthly yoke-fellow. As the child grows towards manhood, his ghost keeps pace with him, and so exactly do they resemble each other in the features, complexions, and aspect, when seen by a third party, that, without the use of prescribed spells, no human observer can distinguish the mortal from the immortal. Nor is this resemblance confined to the personal appearance alone—it is likewise extended to the habiliments. Whether the mortal equips himself in the Highland garb or Lowland costume, the imitative ghost instantly assumes the same attire. The bonnet or the hat, the philibeg or the trews, are equally convenient and agreeable to him; for in this solitary particular he has never been known to dissent from his human partner.

During this period the ghost is supposed either to accompany or precede, at some distance, his human partner (of course invisible to those not possessing the second-sight) in all those multifarious journeys and duties which the mortal performs throughout the course of his eventful life, and the moral utility of the ghost is supposed to consist in propitiating the mortal's undertakings by guarding them from the influence of evil spirits. But, however this may be, it is a well-known fact, that *all* ghosts do not devote the whole of their time to the discharge of this commendable duty. Common fame errs much if those capricious beings do not love their own pleasures more than their partner's interest; and this their negligence is a subject of still deeper regret, when we consider the nature of those practices in which they employ their time.

If the appetites of the modern ghost are better restrained than those of his predecessors were in the "greedy times" we have written of, the mischievous habits he has acquired in lieu of his predecessor's social accomplishments are to some far more calamitous than even *Clashnichd's* practices. It is true, a dose of Highland crowdie would but ill agree with the refined delicacy of the stomach of the former. Such squeamish appetites must look out for more delicate and savoury food. But if the modern ghost does not possess those keen digestive powers which distinguished *Clashnichd*, he inherits all the ill nature of *Ben-Baynac*, without one-third of his might; and we question much if his regard for the fair sex is a bit more tender.

Instead of being the peaceable and industrious associate of his yoke-fellow, it is a common practice with the ghost of the present day to prowl about the country with the laudable intention of committing all the mischief in his power to the friends and acquaintances of his partner. Planting himself in some wild and convenient position, he will open on the ears of the slumbering inhabitants, or the more unfortunate traveller, his wild and unearthly cries, highly gratified, no doubt, at the paralyzing effect they produce on his audience. Of the hideousness of these cries nothing short of auric demonstration can convey an adequate conception. Partaking at once of all that is horrid and unnatural, if any resemblance to them can be figured, we are told it is the "expiring shrieks of a goat under the butcher's knife, or the howling of a dog in a solitary cavern." Proportioned to the strength of the ghost, the cry is loud or faint, and has something so peculiar in it, that the least note never fails to give the hearer a temporary palsy.

But were his practices confined to those comparatively harmless proceedings, the conduct of the ghost would be far less intolerable than it is. His vocal entertainments, however hurtful they sometimes prove to those unfortunate enough to hear them, are not sufficiently iniquitous to satisfy the extent of his malice. Being, no doubt, well disciplined in the noble and fashionable art of pugilism by long experience and practice among his kindred species, never remarkable for their social harmony, he is, perhaps, the best bruiser in the universe, and will never be backward in showing those people who come in his way his expertness in this science. As, however, the greatest part of his human contemporaries are, perhaps, too *strikingly* convinced of his decided superiority, few of them are disposed to hazard a *set-to* with so pithy a combatant, and it is consequently no easy matter for the ghost to fall in with those who are inclined to fight merely for fighting's sake. Finding, therefore, so few willing to quarrel with him in that open and gentlemanlike manner usual in those countries, the fertility of his noddle suggests to him the more indirect or Irish mode of proceeding; and it is to this ingenious mode of raising a row that the Modern Ghost owes the most of his laurels. Presenting himself before the unsuspecting traveller in the servile appearance of a scabbed colt, or some such equally contemptible animal, he will in this guise place himself in the passenger's way, as if to graze by the road's side. Raising his staff, the passenger will very aptly apply it to the colt's back to clear his way, when the malicious animal will instantly retort, and a conflict ensues, in which the unwary transgressor is severely punished for his indiscretion.

In former times, however, and even in recent times, we have heard of some instances where these wanton pugilists proceeded upon more honourable and systematic principles than they do at present. Instead of the dastardly mode of cajoling his adversary into a fight by stratagem, and conquering him by surprise, the warlike bogle of the last century carried about with him flails, cudgels, and such other pithy weapons as were suitable to the spirit of the times,—and on his meeting with a human adventurer who had no objection to become his antagonist, his choice of weapons was left with the latter. Hence it followed that this equitable and impartial mode of proceeding ended not unfrequently to the ghost's great disadvantage; for the *human* bullies of those days were so diligently trained up to the handling of a flail or the wielding of a cudgel, that their ghostly combatants, with all their might and dexterity, have often been the first to propose an armistice. To multiply details of such encounters would be as tedious as they are numerous and similar; a single narrative, communicated to the compiler by the grand-nephew of the person concerned, will, we suppose, be sufficient to confirm our statements.

"Late one night, as my grand-uncle Lachlan *Dhu* Macpherson, who was well known as the best fiddler of his day, was returning home from a ball, at which he had acted as a musician, he had occasion to pass through the once haunted Bog of Torrans. Now, it happened at that time that that Bog was frequented by a huge bogle or ghost, who was of a most mischievous disposition, and took particular pleasure in abusing every traveller who had occasion to pass through the place betwixt the twilight at night and cock-crowing in the morning. Suspecting much that he would also come in for a share of his abuse, my grand-uncle made up his mind, in the course of his progress, to return him any *civilities* which he might think meet to offer him. On arriving on the spot, he found his suspicions were too well grounded; for whom did he see but the Ghost of Bogandoran, apparently ready waiting him, and seeming by his ghastly grin not a little overjoyed at the meeting? Then marching up to my grand-uncle, the bogle clapt a huge club into his hand, and furnishing himself with one of the same dimensions, he put a spittle in his hand, and deliberately commenced the combat. My grand-uncle returned the salute with equal spirit, and so ably did both parties ply their batons, that for a while the issue of the combat was extremely doubtful. At length, however, the fiddler could easily discover that his opponent's vigour was much in the fagging order. Picking up renewed courage in consequence, my grand-uncle, the fiddler, plied the ghost with renovated vigour, and after a stout resistance, in the course of which both parties were seriously handled, the Ghost of Bogandoran thought it prudent to give up the night.

"At the same time, filled, no doubt, with great indignation at this signal defeat, it seems the ghost resolved to re-engage my grand-uncle on some other occasion, under more favourable circumstances. Not long after, as my grand-uncle was returning home quite unattended from another ball in the Braes of the country, he had just entered the hollow of Auldichoish, well known for its 'eery' properties, when lo! who presented himself to his view on the adjacent eminence but his old friend of Bogandoran, advancing as large as the gable of a house, putting himself in the most threatening and fighting attitudes?

"Looking on the very dangerous nature of the ground in which they were met, and feeling no anxiety for a second encounter with a combatant of his weight, in a situation so little desirable, the fiddler would have willingly deferred the settlement of their differences till a more convenient season. He, accordingly, assuming the most submissive aspect in the world, endeavoured to pass by his champion in peace, but in vain. Longing, no doubt, to retrieve the disgrace of his late discomfiture, the bogle instantly seized the fiddler, and attempted with all his might to pull the latter down the precipice, with the diabolical intention, it is supposed, of drowning him in the river Avon below. In this pious design the bogle was happily frustrated by the intervention of some trees which grew in the precipice, and to which my unhappy grand-uncle clung with the zeal of a drowning man. The enraged ghost finding it impossible to extricate him from those friendly trees, and resolving, at all events, to be revenged of him, he fell upon maltreating the fiddler with his hands and feet in the most inhuman manner.

"Such gross indignities my worthy grand-uncle was not accustomed to, and being incensed beyond all measure at the liberties taken by Bogandoran, he resolved again to try his mettle, whether life or death should be the consequence. Having no other weapon wherewith to defend himself but his *biodag*, which, considering the nature of his opponent's constitution, he suspected much would be of little avail to him—I say, in the absence of any other weapon, he sheathed the *biodag* three times in the Ghost of Bogandoran's belly. And what was the consequence? why, to the great astonishment of my courageous forefather, the ghost fell down cold-dead at his feet, and was never more seen or heard of."

Thus it will be seen that in those chivalrous days the stout and energetic sons of Caledonia had courage and prowess enough to cope with those powerful warriors, however unequally matched, with spirit and even with success. In the present effeminate times, we hear of none that will even contend with those miserable scarecrows of the present day. Overcome, more by fear than by force, at the first encounter they throw themselves down, and, like the lamb beneath the fox, tamely submit to the most abusive treatment. Hence, encouraged by those servile submissions, it is almost incredible to what extent those invincible *corps* sometimes carry their audacity. We have heard of not a few of them, who having, in the first place, intruded their company on peaceable travellers on the public road, in the next place offered them the most provoking indignities,—one time piping their unearthly cries into the passenger's ears, at another time tripping him up by the heels, and even committing indecencies which delicacy forbids us to repeat, while the fears and agitation manifested by the traveller constituted a subject of great merriment to the mischievous ghost.

CHAPTER III.
OF THE GHOST IN HIS INTERMEDIATE STATE—HIS SIMILITUDES AND HABITS.

A SHORT time previous to the mortal's death, and when just on the eve of dissolution, the ghost undergoes a striking revolution in his appearance and habits. Seized with the *locked jaw*, and all the other disabilities common to the dead, he then becomes the awful emblem of death in all its similitudes. Attired in a shroud and all the ensigns of the grave, the ghost nocturnally proceeds to the narrow house of his future residence, and there disappears. He is lighted on his way by a pale azure-coloured light, of the size of that emitted by a *tallow* candle, which is of a flickering unsteady nature, sometimes vivid, and sometimes faint, as the mortal inhales and respires his breath; and, in his course towards the grave, he will follow minutely the line of march destined to be followed by his earthly partner's approaching funeral. His pace is slow, and his footsteps imperceptible even to a passenger; who, although he sees clearly all his trappings, cannot discern his mode of travelling. To the naked eye the ghost's visage is not discernible, by reason of the *face-cloth*. There is a very simple process, however, which has been discovered for enabling a spectator to discern whose ghost he is, although we never heard of more than one person who had the hardihood to put the experiment in practice.

It is an admitted fact, in those countries, that a ghost may be recognised, in the appearance of his human partner, on his passing a spectator, by the latter's reversing the cuff of his own coat, or any other part of his raiment, which puts an instant stop to the ghost's career, and clearly exposes him to the recognition of the courageous experimenter.

A sage philosopher, who had long desired an opportunity of practising this bold experiment, found, "late one night," when returning home from a market, a very convenient one. Observing a stout lusty ghost stalking very majestically along the public road, this bold adventurer hesitated not a moment. Clapping himself into a defensive attitude, he reversed his cuff— when, lo! his next-door neighbour's wife was instantly confronted to his face—clad in death's awful apparel—the death-candle lowing in her throat, and mouth full distended. Such an exhibition was too appalling to wish for a long interview; and, accordingly, Donald Doul, the adventurer, made a motion to be off, but in vain. The unhappy man, as if transformed into a stone, could no more move than Lot's wife, and was obliged to stand confronted to his loving companion, both equally sparing of their talk, until the crowing of the cock in the morning. Finding himself then released from his uncomfortable stance, he was about to make the best of his way home, to communicate the result of his experiment, when the friendly wife's ghost thus addressed him: "Donald Doul—Donald Doul—Donald Doul—hear me, and tremble. Great is the hindrance you have caused me this night,—a hindrance for which you should have been severely punished, but for the friendship which formerly subsisted between yourself and my partner. Dare not again to pry into the mysteries of the dead. The time will come when you'll know those secrets." To this poetical harangue Donald Doul made no other reply than a profound obeisance. It is possible, however, the ghost would have proposed a rejoinder, had not a chanticleer, in the adjacent hamlet, emitted his third clarion, at the magic sound of which the wife's ghost fairly took to her heels, leaving Donald Doul to resume his course homewards without further advice. Satisfied of the interesting nature of the occurrence, and that his reputation for courage and veracity would suffer no diminution from the relation, Donald Doul made no secret of what happened. This clearly foretold what speedily took place, the dissolution of the neighbour's wife, (who, by the way, was dangerously ill at the time,) to the great grief of her husband, and the credit of Donald Doul's name.

A short time after the ghost, bearing the death-candle, has thus been seen, the house of the undertaker who is to make the mortal's coffin will be nightly disturbed by the sounds of saws and knocking of hammers, no doubt proceeding from the ghost of the undertaker and his assistants preparing the coffin of the ghost; while invisible messengers will parade the country for necessaries for the ghost's funeral, or foregoing. And a very imposing and interesting spectacle may be looked for.

The mortal resigns his breath, and is about to follow the course of the dead-candle to his new abode, when *Taish na Tialedh*, or the funeral foregoing, takes the road. This is not a paltry spectacle of one ghost, a sight so common in those countries, but a superb assemblage of them, all drest in their best attire, each reflecting lustre on the other. On this occasion, the ghost of every man who is destined to accompany the mortal's funeral will attend, dressed in apparel of the same colour, and mounted on a horse of the same appearance, (if he is to have one,) as his mortal companion on the day of the corporeal interment. On this occasion, too, their characteristic austerity of manners is dispensed with. Mellowed, no doubt, by the generous qualities of the *Usquebaugh*, the jocund laugh, the jest, and repartee, go slapping round, responsive to some mournful dirge proceeding from the defunct's immediate friends and relations.

In the motley group, the ghost of a father or brother is easily recognised by his well-known voice and Sabbath vestment. Nay, the spectator may even recognise himself, if his senses enable him to discriminate, joyous or sorry, as occasion suggests, mingling in the throng. In the middle of the procession the coffin is seen, containing, we presume, the *dead ghost*, circled by mourning relatives; and on the front, flanks, and rear of the burden, the company are likewise seen approaching and retiring, relieving each other by turns. At length, the noise of horses and tongues, horsemen and footmen, mingled indiscriminately together, closes the procession.

The following account of the *foregoing* of the funeral of an illustrious chief, who died some few score of years ago, (witnessed by a man whose veracity was a perfect proverb,) will not, we trust, be unacceptable:

"A smith, who had a large family to provide for, was often necessitated to occupy his smithy till rather a late hour. One night, in particular, as he was turning the key of his smithy door, his notice was attracted to the public road, which lay contiguous to the smithy, by a confusion of sounds, indicative of the approach of a great concourse of people. Immediately there appeared the advanced ranks of a procession, marching four men deep, in tolerable good order, unless occasionally some unaccountable circumstance occasioned the fall of a lusty fellow, as if he had been shot by a twenty-four pounder. Thunderstruck at the nature and number of the marvellous procession, the smith, honest man, reclined his back to the door, witnessing a continuation of the same procession for nearly an hour, without discovering any thing further of the character of those who composed it, than that they betokened a repletion of the *Usquebaugh*. At length, the appearance of the hearse and its awful ensigns, together with the succeeding line of coaches, developed the nature of the concern. It was then that the smith's knees began to smite each other, and his hair to stand on an end. The recent demise of this venerable chieftain confirmed his conviction of its being a *Taish*, and a very formidable one too. Not choosing to see the rear, he directed his face homewards, whither he fled with the swiftness of younger years, and was not backward in favouring his numerous acquaintances with a full and particular account of the whole scene. This induced many honest people to assume the smithy door as their stance of observation on the day of the funeral, which took place a few days after; and, to his honour be it told, every circumstance detailed by the smith in his relation accurately happened, even to the decanting of two dogs, and this established the smith's veracity in all time thereafter."

Akin to this are all the relations of those good people whose evil destiny it has been to fall in with those ghostly processions, some of whom having inadvertently involved themselves into the crowd, were repulsed in every attempt to extricate themselves, until carried along, nobody knows how far, by the tumultuous rabble, who seemed to enjoy themselves vastly at the standing hair, protruding eyes, and awry visage of the unconscious intruder.

In concluding this part of our subject, it is hardly necessary to add, that in two or three days after the ghostly procession, the human or corporeal procession will succeed it, following most minutely and accurately every course, winding, and turn taken by the foregoing, while the dress, conversation, and every other incident attending the company will be precisely the same.

CHAPTER IV.
OF THE GHOST IN HIS POST-EXISTENT STATE.

IT might, no doubt, be readily supposed by the ingenious reader, that the mortal's decease should be the term of dissolution assigned to the copartnery connection subsisting between the mortal and his ghost, as it generally terminates every other engagement into which the people of this world enter. The event, however, only serves to blend their interests still more strictly together. Whatever doubt may exist as to the ghost's attention to his partner's worldly interests in his lifetime, his solicitude for his spiritual interest, after the mortal's death, is universally acknowledged. He then becomes the sole means of remedying past errors, and obtaining redress for past injuries. To enable one fully to appreciate a ghost's utility in the "land of the leal," he must acquaint himself with the nature of the life which the defunct led, whether regular in his habits and moral in his life, or otherwise, and the particular situation of his affairs at death. If, for instance, a man falls suddenly, like a tree in a storm, whatever may be the situation or circumstances in which he happens to drop, so he must lie. In this respect, then, the peculiar advantage of the Highlander over his Lowland neighbour becomes perfectly apparent. Through the medium of a faithful ghost and a confidential friend, transactions, as intricate and ravelled as those of the Laird of Coul, can be easily simplified and assorted.

No man should, therefore, be surprised, if the ghost of some departed friend should take an opportunity of saluting him, and for his own sake he should also lose no time in enabling the awful emissary to declare the purpose of his mission; whoever will defer doing so only increases his own misery, and it is a task, however uncomfortable, that is sacredly due to departed friendship; for how many, by yielding to the influence of cowardly fear, have exposed themselves and their household to those nocturnal rackets sometimes raised by those disappointed ambassadors, whereas a little resolution would not only have averted it, but have also greatly conduced to the repose and quietude of an old and esteemed acquaintance. The following statement of a circumstance which, we are told, happened in Strathspey not a great many years ago, will best enforce this counsel:

"Not many years ago there lived in Kincardine of Strathspey a poor man, who contracted a severe and sudden illness, which, to the great grief of his family, terminated in his death. From the suddenness of the honest man's call, he had not time to settle his affairs, and this circumstance, it seems, as might have been supposed, caused him no small disquietude in the eternal world. He wished, in particular, to have had an axe and a whisky barrel, which he had borrowed of a friend, restored to him; for iron, you must know, in such cases, is very bad. In order, therefore, to have this matter adjusted, the dead man commissioned his ghost to wait on a particular friend to disclose to him the circumstance, not doubting in the least but the friend would have bestowed his best attention on the subject. The faithful ghost lost no time in proceeding to get the object of his mission accomplished, which, however, turned out rather a difficult undertaking, for it was no easy matter for the ghost to procure a conference with the friend on the business. One glimpse of the former never failed to communicate to the latter the feet of a roe, nor could all his dexterity bring the matter to a bearing. At length, exasperated by a long course of night watching and useless travelling, the wily commissioner had recourse to an expedient which ultimately effected his purpose. As soon as the sun went down every evening, the ghost opened a cannonade of bricks and stones upon the unhappy friend and the inmates of his house, which did not terminate till cock-crowing in the morning; and so expert an archer was this pawky ghost, that he scarcely ever missed an aim, while every stroke would kill a bullock. Smarting under the effect of this unseasonable chastisement, the friend and his family raised the most outrageous clamour at their unaccountable misfortune, which induced some of their neighbours nightly to assemble in considerable bodies to protect them from this nocturnal warfare. But the wily ghost, far from relaxing his operations on that account, only plied them with additional vigour, sparing neither sex nor age in his sweeping career. All sorts of missiles announced themselves, rebounding on the shoulders of the protectors as well as the protected, the pithy weight of which, and the unaccountable manner in which they were flung, convinced the sufferers they were not flung by mortal hand. All the acquaintances of the friend, therefore, urged on him to challenge the invisible demon who thus savagely persecuted him at the hour of midnight, in order to afford the latter an opportunity of explaining his business, and the reason of his cruel and unchristian conduct. But this advice the friend of the deceased was disposed to consider a dernier resort, and one that required some cool consideration. At length, rendered quite desperate by a series of unparalleled persecutions, which rendered him as thin in body as a silver sixpence, the goodman came to a final determination to call the ghost to account the very first opportunity, for his mean and pusillanimous attacks on himself and poor family. Accordingly, one night, on receiving a tart pill on the cheek, which gave him an ear-ache, and which wonderfully improved his courage, the goodman marched forth, with a mixture of rage and fear, demanding of the unfeeling ghost, in a voice resembling the falling notes of the gamut, 'Wha-a-t i-i-s you-r bus-n-ess wi' m-my ho-use a-

and fa-fa-fa-mi-ly?' The ghost instantly appeared happy to answer the question; but, ere he could do so, it was necessary to go through a ceremony, which is no less curious than it is disagreeable to the feelings of the parties concerned. This ceremony consists in the *mortal's* embracing the ghost, and raising his feet from the ground, so as to allow the wind to pass between the soles of his feet and the ground, which enables the tongue-tied ghost to speak a volume. What was then to be done in this particular case? Encouraged by the eloquent cheers and arguments held forth to him, through the crevices of his house, by his anxious family, he made several attempts to encircle the awful emissary in his arms, which, by a sort of mechanical motion, receded from the embrace; and it was not without great difficulty he could persuade himself to give a friendly embrace to this mischievous ghost; this, however, he did at last,—seizing him as he would a bush of thorns. The ghost's long-locked jaws now began to speak in so sepulchral a tone as to palsy all who heard it. The friend of the deceased promised strict attention to all the ghost's injunctions, upon which he evanished in a flame of fire, leaving the unhappy man scarce able to totter to his chair. A minute compliance with all his instructions rendered a second visit from the ghost unnecessary—and this was no small matter of comfort to the friend."

This frigid display of a Highlandman's courage will appear very contemptible when compared to the undaunted resolution of the female alluded to in the following story:

"About forty or fifty years ago, a native of Strathdown, whose manner of living (like that of other folks) did not qualify him for a sudden death, was unfortunately drowned in the following manner: While in the act of cutting down a tree, in a steep precipice pending over the river Avon, he slipped his footing—fell headlong into the abyss below, and rose no more. His lamentable fate was speedily discovered, his body interred, and his affairs arranged in the best possible order. Time, the parent of oblivion, soon rendered his name extinct among the living, and he was no longer heard of; when, on a certain day, in the height of it, the deceased appeared in his human likeness at the window of a female friend. On the woman's exhibiting some surprise and terror at his appearance, the drowned man called to her to fear nothing, but to come forth and speak with him,—for it seems he had been enabled to speak without the '*dead-lift.*' The honest woman suspecting, no doubt, that, if she did not go out to him, he would make the best of his way to her, obeyed his summons; and, in the course of a long convoy she gave him, he divulged to her several acts of misconduct he had been guilty of towards an old master and some others, which disturbed much his repose. Anxious, no doubt, to get rid of his company, she promised to exert the best of her endeavours to atone for his misconduct, on condition he would leave her, and never again renew his visit,—a promise which she faithfully performed, and the dead friend gave her no farther trouble."

But the settlement of unassorted affairs, after death, is not the only thing in which the ghost is extremely useful. As an ambassador ever ready to discharge any piece of useful service—such as appeasing the unavailing grief of lamenting relatives—he is ever ready and expert, and the delicate manner in which the ghost sometimes executes this commission indicates that he is far more friendly and conciliatory in his behaviour when *dead* than he was when alive. Sometimes, but rarely, he leaves his abode to benefit an old acquaintance or friend of his partner; but it will no doubt be done at the instigation of the devoted latter. We present the particulars of a favour of this sort conferred on an inhabitant of Strathspey, no doubt a long time ago, which deserved a better return than what the ghost at first met with.

"Engaged one night in the arrangement of his farming affairs, a certain farmer, living in the parish of Abernethy, was a good deal surprised at seeing an old acquaintance, who had a considerable time previously departed this life, entering quite coolly at his dwelling-house door. Instead of following his old acquaintance into his house, to receive an explanation from himself of the marvellous circumstance, his curiosity led him into the church-yard where his friend was buried, and which was near by, to see if he had actually risen from the dead. On examination, he not only found the grave, but also the coffin *wide open*, which left no doubt on his mind of the reality of the vision which he thought had deluded his sight. Making the sign of the cross on the grave, he returned to his house, not caring whether he found his friend before him or not. He was not, however, to be seen; but, in the course of a short time, he returned, and upbraided the farmer for his improper interference with his grave, explaining to him the cause of his resurrection. It appeared that a scabbed stirk, which had a greedy custom of prowling about the doors, seeking what he might devour, thief-like entering the dwelling-house in the absence of the family, and, finding no better subject of entertainment, attacked the straw in the cradle which stood by the fireside, and in which his only child was sleeping at the time. The tugging of the stirk at the straw would have inevitably overturned the cradle and the child into the fire but for the generous interposition of the ghost. The farmer expressed his most grateful acknowledgments for so signal an instance of his kindness; and immediately retraced his steps to the grave, on which he made a counter-sign to that which he formerly made, and the good-hearted ghost obtained admission into his dreary abode."

But these are not all the ghost's useful qualities. He possesses another very important one in this unchristian and uncharitable age, in which the repositories of the dead are exposed to the nocturnal spoliation of the ruthless resurrectionist. It is vain for the church-sexton to plant *steel-traps* and *spring-guns* in the field of his labours,—the wily depredator will contrive to elude them all when the vigilant watchman is wanted to direct them. To show the vigilance of this agent's attention to his own interest, and that of his friends, on such occasions, take the following narration:—

"There was at one time a woman, who lived in Camp-del-more of Strathavon, whose cattle were seized with a murrain, or some such fell disease, which ravaged the neighbourhood at the time, carrying off great numbers of them daily. All the *forlorn fires and hallowed waters* failed of their customary effects; and she was at length told by the wise people whom she consulted on the occasion, that it was evidently the effect of some infernal agency, the power of which could not be destroyed by any other means than the never-failing specific—the juice of a *dead head* from the church-yard,—a nostrum certainly very difficult to be procured, considering the head must needs be abstracted from a grave in the hour of midnight. Being, however, a woman of a stout heart and strong faith, native feelings of delicacy towards the blessed sanctuary of the dead had more weight in restraining her for some time from resorting to this desperate remedy than those of fear. At length, seeing that her bestial stock would soon be completely annihilated by the destructive career of the disease, the wife of Camp-del-more resolved to put the experiment in practice, whatever the result might be. Accordingly, having, with considerable difficulty, engaged a neighbouring woman to be her companion in this hazardous expedition, they set out, about midnight, for the parish church-yard, distant about a mile and a half from her residence, to execute her determination. On arriving at the church-yard, her companion, whose courage was not so notable, appalled by the gloomy prospect before her, refused to enter among the habitations of the dead. She, however, agreed to remain at the gate till her friend's business was accomplished. This circumstance, however, did not stagger our heroine's resolution. She, with the greatest coolness and intrepidity, proceeded towards what she supposed an old grave,—took down her spade, and commenced her operations. After a good deal of toil she arrived at the object of her labour. Raising the first head, or rather skull, that came in her way, she was about to make it her own property, when, lo! a hollow, wild, sepulchral voice exclaimed, 'That is *my* head—let it alone!' Not wishing to dispute the claimant's title to this head, and supposing she could be otherwise provided, she very good-naturedly returned it, and took up another. 'That is my father's head,' bellowed the same voice. Wishing, if possible, to avoid disputes, the wife of Camp-del-more took up another head, when the same voice instantly started a claim to it as his grand-father's head. 'Well,' replied the wife, nettled at her disappointments, 'although it were your grand-mother's head, you shan't get it till I am done with it.'—'What do you say, you limmer?'

says the ghost, starting up in his awry habiliments; 'What do you say, you limmer?' repeated he in a great rage. 'By the great oath, you had better leave my grand-father's head.' Upon matters coming this length, the wily wife of Camp-del-more thought it proper to assume a more conciliatory aspect. Telling the claimant the whole particulars of the predicament in which she was placed by the foresaid calamity, she promised faithfully, that, if his Honour would only allow her to carry off his grand-father's skull, or head, in a peaceable manner, she would restore it again when done with it. Here, after some communing, they came to an understanding, and she was allowed to take the head along with her, on condition she should restore it before cock-crowing, under the heaviest penalties.

"On coming out of the church-yard, and looking for her companion, she had the mortification to find her 'without a mouthful of breath in her body;' for, on hearing the dispute between her friend and the guardian of the grave, and suspecting much that she was likely to share the unpleasant punishments with which he threatened her friend, at the bare recital of them she fell down in a faint, from which it was no easy matter to recover her. This proved no small inconvenience to Camp-del-more's wife, as there were not above two hours to elapse ere she had to return the head in terms of her agreement. Taking her friend upon her back, she carried her up a steep acclivity to the nearest adjoining house, where she left her for the night; then repaired home with the utmost speed—made *dead bree* of the *dead head*, and, ere the appointed time had expired, she restored the head to its guardian, and placed the grave in its former condition. It is needless to add, that, as a reward for her exemplary courage, the '*bree*' had its desired effect—the cattle speedily recovered—and, so long as she retained any of it, all sorts of diseases were of short duration."

SAFEGUARDS FROM GHOSTS.

HAVING now briefly described the leading features of a ghost's character in those countries, we shall close our account of him by annexing a few of those safeguards which protect us from those wanton encounters and impertinent interferences which we have related, and which must be far from being palatable to the more effeminate inhabitants of the Highland mountains at the present day.

One simple plan of obtaining perfect security from supernatural agents of any kind is, (whenever we apprehend the approach or presence of a ghost,) to repeat certain words, which can be taught by any wise patriarch or matron, the powerful charm of which instantly repercusses the ghost back to his own proper abode, and, for the time, defeats all his machinations. Note—If in the house, the words must be repeated three times behind the door. A ghost then can neither enter at the door, window, nor any other crevice of the house. The operation of the words is like that of an infeftment, which, taken on one part of the property, affects the whole. Were it not for this grand discovery, vain would be the attempt of any man to bar out a ghost as he might do a *mortal*. A ghost can enter in at the key-hole—nay, even through the wall of the house, if there is no other caveat to arrest him in his career.

Another safeguard consists in forming a piece of the *rowan tree* into the shape of a cross with a red thread. This cross you will insert between the lining and cloth of your garment, and, so long as it lasts, neither ghost nor witch shall ever interfere with you.

PART II.
Fairies.

There are fairies, and brownies, and shades Amazonian,

Of harper, and sharper, and old Cameronian;

Some small as pigmies, some tall as a steeple:

The spirits are all gone as mad as the people.

HOGG.

CHAPTER I.
ORIGIN AND GENEALOGY OF THE FAIRIES.

THOUGH the ghost is confessedly entitled to no small degree of consideration from his intimate connection with our own species, no one will pretend to deny that the fairy is a character whose *greatness of descent* renders him equally interesting and respectable. The genealogy of the ghost can no doubt be traced back to the earliest ages of the world, and it is pretty certain that he has been amongst the first of its inhabitants; still, on the score of antiquity, he cannot pretend to compete with the fairy, who, it seems, existed long before the world itself. The origin and descent of the fairies, which had so long proved such knotty subjects of controversy in other quarters of the kingdom, are points which have been finally settled and disposed of in these countries. No doubt now remains, in the minds of those who have bestowed any attention on the important subject, of there being those unhappy angels whose diabolical deeds produced their expulsion from Paradise. In support of this rational theory, the wise men of the day never fail to quote the highest authority. Scripture, they say, tells us those angels were cast down; and although, indeed, it does not mention to what place, sad experience proves the fact, that the Highland mountains received an ample share of them. Here, wandering up and down, like the hordes of Tartary, they pitch their camp where spoil is most plentiful; and taking advantage of the obstinate incredulity of some of their human neighbours, contrive to make themselves perfectly comfortable at the latter's expense. To dispel any doubt that may remain on the mind of the reader as to the soundness of this doctrine, we present him with the following particulars:

"Not long since, as a pious clergyman was returning home, after administering spiritual consolation to a dying member of his flock, it was late of the night, and he had to pass through a good deal of *uncanny* ground. He was, however, a good and conscientious minister of the gospel, and feared not all the spirits in the country. On his reaching the end of a lake which stretched alongst the road-side for some distance, he was a good deal surprised to have his attention arrested by the most melodious strains of music. Overcome by pleasure and curiosity, the minister coolly sat down to listen to the harmonious sounds, and try what new discoveries he could make with regard to their nature and source. He had not sitten many minutes when he could distinguish the approach of the music, and also observe a light in the direction from whence it proceeded, gliding across the lake towards him. Instead of taking to his heels, as any faithless wight would have done, the pastor, fearless, determined to await the issue of the phenomenon. As the light and music drew near, the clergyman could at length distinguish an object resembling a human being walking on the surface of the water, attended by a group of diminutive musicians, some of them bearing lights, and others of them instruments of music, on which they continued to perform those melodious strains which first attracted his attention. The leader of the band dismissed his attendants, landed on the beach, and afforded the minister the amplest opportunities of examining his appearance. He was a little primitive-looking grey-headed man, clad in the most grotesque habit he ever witnessed, and such as led the venerable minister all at once to suspect his real character. He walked up to the minister, whom he saluted with great grace, offering an apology for his intrusion. The pastor returned his compliments, and, without farther explanation, invited the mysterious stranger to sit down by his side. The invitation was complied with, upon which the minister proposed the following question: '*Who art thou, stranger, and from whence?*' To this question the fairy, with downcast eye, replied, that he was one of those sometimes called '*Doane Shee*, or men of peace, or good men, though the reverse of this title was a more fit appellation for them. Originally angelic in his nature and attributes, and once a sharer of the indescribable joys of the regions of light, he was seduced by Satan to join him in his mad conspiracies; and as a punishment for his transgression, he was cast down from those regions of bliss, and was now doomed, along with millions of fellow-sufferers, to wander through seas and mountains, until the coming of the great day; what their fate would be then they could not divine, but they apprehended the worst. And,' continued he, turning to the minister, with great anxiety, 'the object of my present intrusion on you is to learn your opinion, as an eminent divine, as to our final condition on that dreadful day.' Here the venerable pastor entered upon a long conversation with the fairy, (the particulars of which we shall be excused for omitting,) touching the principles of faith and repentance. Receiving rather unsatisfactory answers to his questions, the minister desired the '*Sheech*' to repeat after him the Paternoster; in attempting to do which, it was not a little remarkable that he could not repeat the word '*art*,' but '*wert*,' in heaven. Inferring from every circumstance that their fate was extremely precarious, the minister resolved not to puff the fairies up with presumptuous and perhaps groundless expectations. Accordingly, addressing himself to the unhappy fairy, who was all anxiety to know the nature of his sentiments, the reverend gentleman told him that he could not take it upon him to give them any hopes of pardon, as their crime was of so deep a hue as scarcely to admit of it. On this the unhappy fairy uttered a shriek of despair, plunged headlong into the loch, and the minister resumed his course to his home."

CHAPTER II.
SIMILITUDE OF THE FAIRY.

OF all the different species of supernatural tribes which inhabit those countries, none of them could ever vie with the fairy community for personal elegance. Indeed, this seems to be the only remaining vestige they possess of their primitive character. Though generally low in stature, they are exceedingly well proportioned, and prepossessing in their persons. The females, in particular, are said to be the most enchanting beings in the world, and far beyond what the liveliest fancy can paint. Eyes sparkling as the brightest of the stars, or the polished gem of Cairngorm,—cheeks in which the whiteness of the snow and red of the reddan are blended with the softness of the Cannoch down,—lips like the coral, and teeth like the ivory,—a redundant luxuriance of auburn hair hanging down the shoulders in lovely ringlets, and a gainly simplicity of dress, always of the colour of green, are prominent features in the description of a Highland fairy nymph.

But while we agree in some measure with our fellow historians who have described the fairy race as they exist in other quarters of the country, in so far as regards their personal beauty, we widely differ from those historians as to the splendour of their dress as exhibited in the character of the Highland fairies. Instead of the gorgeous habiliments of "white and gold dropped with diamonds, and coats of the threads of gold," which we are told are worn by those more luxurious and refined fairies living within the sphere of splendour and fashion in the Lowlands of Scotland; the Highland fairies, more thrifty and less voluptuous, clothe themselves in plain worsted green, not woven by the "*shuttle of Iris*," but by the greasy shuttle of some Highland weaver. This description, let it be understood, however, applies only to the portion of them inhabiting *terra firma*; for the dress of those whose lot it was to fall in the deep is of a very different nature, consisting entirely of seal-skins, and such other *marine* apparel as is most suitable and appropriate to their element.

The following story will throw some light upon the manners and *habits* of this portion of the fairy tribes.

There was once upon a time a man who lived on the northern coasts, not far from "*Taigh Jan Crot Callow*," and he gained his livelihood by catching and killing fish, of all sizes and denominations. He had a particular liking to the killing of those wonderful beasts, half dog half fish, called "Roane," or Seals, no doubt because he got a long price for their skins, which are not less curious than they are valuable. The truth is, that most of these animals are neither dogs nor cods, but downright fairies, as this narration will show; and, indeed, it is easy for any man to convince himself of the fact by a simple examination of his *tobacco-spluichdan*,—for the dead skins of those beings are never the same for four-and-twenty hours together. Sometimes the "*spluichdan*" will erect its bristles almost perpendicularly, while, at other times, it reclines them even down; one time it resembles a bristly sow, at another time a *sleekit cat*; and what dead skin, except itself, could perform such cantrips? Now, it happened one day, as this notable fisher had returned from the prosecution of his calling, that he was called upon by a man who seemed a great stranger, and who said he had been dispatched for him by a person who wished to contract for a quantity of seal-skins, and that it was necessary for the fisher to accompany him (the stranger) immediately to see the person who wished to contract for the skins, as it was necessary that he should be served that evening. Happy in the prospect of making a good bargain, and never suspecting any duplicity in the stranger, he instantly complied. They both mounted a steed belonging to the stranger, and took the road with such velocity that, although the direction of the wind was towards their back, yet the fleetness of their movement made it appear as if it had been in their faces. On reaching a stupendous precipice which overhung the sea, his guide told him they had now reached the point of their destination. "Where is the person you spoke of?" inquired the astonished seal-killer. "You shall see that presently," replied the guide. With that they immediately alighted, and, without allowing the seal-killer much time to indulge the frightful suspicions that began to pervade his mind, the stranger seized him with irresistible force, and plunged headlong with the seal-killer into the sea. After sinking down—down—nobody knows how far, they at length reached a door, which, being open, led them into a range of apartments, filled with inhabitants—not people, but seals, who could nevertheless speak and feel like human folk; and how much was the seal-killer surprised to find that he himself had been unconsciously transformed into the like image! If it were not so, he would probably have died, from the want of breath. The nature of the poor fisher's thoughts may be more easily conceived than described. Looking on the nature of the quarters into which he was landed, all hopes of escape from them appeared wholly chimerical, whilst the degree of comfort and length of life which the barren scene promised him were far from being flattering. The "Roane," who all seemed in very low spirits, appeared to feel for him, and endeavoured to soothe the distress which he evinced, by the amplest assurances of personal safety. Involved in sad meditation on his evil fate, he was quickly roused from his stupor, by his guide's producing a huge gully or joctaleg, the object of which he supposed was to put an end to all his earthly cares. Forlorn as was his situation, however, he did not wish to be killed; and, apprehending instant destruction, he fell down, and earnestly implored for mercy. The poor generous animals did not mean him any harm, however much his former conduct deserved it; and he was accordingly desired to pacify himself, and cease his cries. "Did you ever see that knife before?" says the stranger to the fisher. The latter instantly recognising his own knife, which he had that day stuck into a seal, and with which it made its escape, acknowledged it was formerly his own, for what would be the use of denying it? "Well!" rejoins the guide, "the apparent seal, which made away with it, is my father, who lies dangerously ill ever since, and no means could stay his fleeting breath, without your aid. I have been obliged to resort to the artifice I have practised to bring you hither, and I trust that my filial duty to my father will readily operate my excuse." Having said this, he led into another apartment the trembling seal-killer, who expected every minute a return of his own favour to the father; and here he found the identical seal, with which he had the encounter in the morning, suffering most grievously from a tremendous cut in its hind-quarter. The seal-killer was then desired, with his hand, to cicatrize the wound; upon doing which, it immediately healed, and the seal arose from its bed in perfect health. Upon this, the scene changed from mourning to rejoicing,—all was mirth and glee. Very different, however, were the feelings of the unfortunate seal-catcher, expecting, no doubt, to be a seal for the remainder of his life, until his late guide accosted him as follows: "Now, sir, you are at liberty to return to your wife and family, to whom I am about to conduct you; but it is on this express condition, to which you must bind yourself by a solemn oath, viz., that you shall never maim or kill a seal in all your lifetime hereafter." To this condition, hard as it was, he joyfully acceded; and the oath being administered in all due form, he bade his new acquaintance most heartily and sincerely a long farewell. Taking hold of his guide, they issued from the place, and swam up—up— till they regained the surface of the sea; and, landing at the said stupendous pinnacle, they found their former riding steed ready for a second canter. The guide breathed upon the fisher, and they became like men. They mounted their horse; and fleet as was their course towards the precipice or pinnacle, their return from it was doubly swift; and the honest seal-killer was laid down at his own door-cheek, where his guide made him such a present as would have almost reconciled him to another similar expedition, and such as rendered his loss of profession, in so far as regarded the seals, a far less intolerable hardship than he had at first contemplated it.

CHAPTER III.
OF THE FAIRIES AS A COMMUNITY—
THEIR POLITICAL PRINCIPLES AND
INGENIOUS HABITS.

FROM the description the reader may have seen of the fairy community in general, as drawn in the works of the eminent writers of the day, he may have been led to form very erroneous estimates not only of the dress of the *Highland* fairies, but also of their political economy and government.

There are few who have not heard of the illustrious and divine beauty of the Queen of the Fairies, and the splendid and dazzling courts with which her majesty is surrounded on all occasions of intercourse with the inhabitants of this world. It appears, however, from all that the compiler can learn, that the empire of Queen Mab, like that of the renowned Cæsar, never was extended to the northern side of the Grampians, for she is entirely unknown in those countries. Indeed, it is believed that the Highland fairies acknowledge no distinctions of this sort. As there were originally none such amongst them in Paradise, so they are not disposed to create any on earth,—and a more complete republic never was.

It is true, Satan, no doubt, exercises a sort of impotent chieftainship over them as his once rebellious confederates,—but, it is believed, his laws and his edicts are as much despised by them as those of the Great Mogul. In spite of all his power and policy, like the Israelites of old, each does what is right in his own eyes; and, unless on a Halloween, or such occasion of state, they may submit to a pageant review more from motives of vanity than of loyalty, Auld Nick's ancient sovereignty over the fairy community in this land of freedom has fallen into desuetude.

The fairies are a very ingenious people. As may be expected from the nature of their origin and descent, they are possessed of very superior intellectual powers, which they know well enough how to apply to useful purposes. Nor are they so vain of their abilities as to scorn to direct them to the prosecution of those more ignoble employments, on which the politer part of mankind commonly look down with contempt. Whether this condescension, on the part of the fairy, be more the result of choice or necessity, it is hard for us to determine; but certain it is, that few communities can boast of a more numerous or more proficient body of artisans. We are told, indeed, by some of those well acquainted with their manners, that every individual fairy combines all the necessary arts in his own person—that he is his own weaver, his own tailor, and his own shoemaker. Whether this is truly the case public opinion is rather divided; but all our informants concur in this conclusion—that by far the greater number of them understand well enough those several callings; and the expertness they display in handling the shuttle, the needle, and the awl, evidently demonstrate their practical knowledge of these implements. In support of this conclusion, we have the authority of a decent old man, whose veracity, on subjects of this description, has never been questioned in the district in which he lived, who favoured the compiler with the following narration:

"My great-grandfather, (peace to his manes!) who was by profession a weaver, and, by the bye, a very honest man, though I should not say it, was waked one night from his midnight sleep by a tremendous noise. On looking '*out over*' the bed, to see whence it proceeded, he was not a little astonished to find the house full of operative fairies, who, with the greatest familiarity, had made free with his manufacturing implements. Having provided themselves with a large sack of wool,—from whence it came they best knew,—they were actively employed in converting it into cloth. While one teethed it, another carded it; while another span it, another wove it; while another dyed it, another pressed it; while the united bustle of their several operations, joined to the exclamations uttered by each expressive of his avocation, created a clamour truly intolerable to the gudeman of the house, with whom they used so unacceptable a freedom. So diligent were they, that long ere day they decamped with a web of green cloth, consisting of fifty ells and more, without even thanking my venerable grandfather for the use of his machinery."

Another narrative, with which we were favoured, related the activity of a fairy shoemaker, who sewed a pair of shoes for a "*mountain shepherd*" during the time the latter mealed a bicker of pottage for them. And another narrative related the expertness of a fairy *barber*, who shaved an acquaintance so effectually with no sharper a razor than the palm of his hand, that he never afterwards required to undergo the same operation. These, and a number of equally creditable stories, confirm their transcendent superiority as artisans over any other class of people in Christendom.

Nor in the more honourable and learned professions are they less dexterous. As architects they stand quite unrivalled. To prove their excellence in this art we have only to consider the durability of their habitations. Some of these, it is said, have outlived the ravages of time and vicissitudes of weather for some thousand years, without sustaining any other injury than the suffocation of the smoke-vents—defects which could no doubt be repaired with little trouble. But as the relics of former ages receive additional interest from their rude and ruinous appearance, so must these monuments of fairy genius excite in the breasts of the community the most profound sentiments of respect and veneration.

Nor are these the only monuments remaining calculated to perpetuate their excellence as architects and engineers,—there are others of too lasting and extraordinary a character to escape the notice of the traditional historian. We allude to those stupendous superstructures built by the fairies under the auspices of that distinguished arch-architect Mr. Michael Scott, which sufficiently demonstrate the skill of the designer and the ability of the workmen. As the history of this celebrated character (rendered not the less interesting by the notices of him written by the Minstrel of Minstrels) is not yet quite complete, we shall make no apology for submitting to the reader the following anecdotes of his life, which we have collected in the course of our peregrinations.

MICHAEL SCOTT.

IN the early part of Michael Scott's life he was in the habit, as is not yet uncommon with northern tradesmen, of emigrating annually to the Scottish metropolis, for the purpose of being employed in his capacity of mason. One time, as himself and two companions were journeying to the place of their destination for a similar object, they had occasion to pass over a high hill, the name of which is not mentioned, but supposed to be one of the Grampians, and being fatigued with climbing, they sat down to rest themselves. They had no sooner done so than they were warned to take to their heels by the hissing of a large serpent, which they observed revolving itself towards them with great velocity. Terrified at the sight, Michael's two companions fled, while he, on the contrary, resolved to encounter the serpent. The appalling monster approached Michael Scott with distended mouth and forked tongue; and, throwing itself into a coil at his feet, was raising its head to inflict a mortal sting, when Michael, with one stroke of his stick, severed its body into three pieces. Having rejoined his affrighted comrades, they resumed their journey; and, on arriving at the next public-house, it being late, and the travellers being weary, they took up their quarters at it for the night. In the course of the night's conversation, recurrence was naturally had to Michael's recent exploit with the serpent, when the landlady of the house, who was remarkable for her "arts," happened to be present. Her curiosity appeared much excited by the conversation; and, after making some inquiries regarding the colour of the serpent, which she was told was *white*, she offered any of them, that would procure her the middle piece, such a tempting reward, as induced one of the party instantly to go for it. The distance was not very great; and, on reaching the spot, he found the middle and tail piece in the place where Michael left them; but the head piece was gone, it is supposed, to a contiguous stream, to which the serpent is said always to resort, after an encounter with the human race, and, on immersing itself into the water, "like polypus asunder cut," it again regenerates and recovers. On the other hand, it is a circumstance deserving the attention of the medical world, that should an individual, unfortunate enough to be bitten by this galling enemy of mankind, reach the water before the serpent, his recovery from the effects of the calamity is equally indubitable.

The landlady, on receiving the piece, which still vibrated with life, seemed highly gratified at her acquisition; and, over and above the promised reward, regaled her lodgers very plentifully with the choicest dainties in her house. Fired with curiosity to know the purpose for which the serpent was intended, the wily Michael Scott was immediately seized with a severe fit of indisposition,—an excruciating colic, the pains of which could only be alleviated by continual exposure to the fire, the warmth of which, he affirmed, was in the highest degree beneficial to him.

Never suspecting Michael Scott's hypocrisy, and naturally supposing that a person so severely indisposed should feel very little curiosity about the contents of any cooking utensils which might lie around the fire, the landlady consented to his desire of being allowed to recline all night along the fireside. As soon as the other inmates of the house were retired to bed, the landlady resorted to her darling occupation; and, in this feigned state of indisposition, Michael had a favourable opportunity of watching most scrupulously all her actions, through the key-hole of a door leading to the next apartment where she was. He could see the rites and ceremonies with which the serpent was put into an oven, along with many mysterious ingredients. After which, the unsuspicious landlady placed it by the fireside, where lay our distressed traveller, to stove till the morning.

Once or twice, in the course of the night, the "wife of the change-house," under pretence of inquiring for her sick lodger, and administering to him some renovating cordials, the beneficial effects of which he gratefully acknowledged, took occasion to dip her finger in her saucepan, upon which the cock, perched on his roost, crowed aloud. All Michael's sickness could not prevent him from considering very inquisitively the landlady's cantrips, and particularly the influence of the sauce upon the crowing of the cock. Nor could he dissipate some inward desires he felt to follow her example. At the same time that he suspected that Satan had a hand in the pye, yet he liked very much to be at the bottom of the concern; and thus his reason and his curiosity clashed against each other for the space of several hours. At length, passion, as is too often the case, became the conqueror. Michael, too, dipt his finger in the sauce, and applied it to the tip of his tongue, and immediately the cock perched on the *spardan* announced the circumstance in a mournful clarion. Instantly his mind received a new light to which he was formerly a stranger, and the astonished dupe of a landlady now found it her interest to admit her sagacious lodger into a knowledge of the remainder of her secrets.

Endowed with the knowledge of "*good and evil*," and all the "*second sights*" that can be acquired, Michael left his lodgings in the morning, with the philosopher's stone in his pocket. By daily perfecting his supernatural attainments, by new series of discoveries, he was more than a match for Satan himself. Having seduced some thousands of Satan's best workmen into his employment, he trained them up so successfully to the architective business, and inspired them with such industrious habits, that he was more than sufficient for the architectural work of the empire. To establish this assertion, we need only refer to some remains of his workmanship still existing north of the Grampians, some of them stupendous bridges built by him in one short night, with no other visible agents than two or three workmen.

As the following anecdote is so applicable to our purpose, we shall submit it to the reader as a specimen of the expertness of Mr. Scott and his agents.

On one occasion, work was getting scarce, as might have been naturally expected, and his workmen, as they were wont, flocked to his doors, perpetually exclaiming, Work! work! work! Continually annoyed by their incessant entreaties, he called out to them in derision to go and make a dry road from Fortrose to Arderseir over the Moray Firth. Immediately their cry ceased, and as Mr. Scott supposed it wholly impracticable for them to execute his order, he retired to rest, laughing most heartily at the chimerical sort of employment he had given to his industrious workmen. Early in the morning, however, he got up and took a walk down at the break of day to the shore, to divert himself at the fruitless labours of his zealous workmen. But on reaching the spot, what was his astonishment to find the formidable piece of work allotted to them only a few hours before almost quite finished. Seeing the great damage the commercial class of the community would sustain from the operation, he ordered them to demolish the most part of their work; leaving, however, the point of Fortrose to show the traveller to this day the wonderful exploit of Michael Scott's fairies.

On being thus again thrown out of employment, their former clamour was resumed, nor could Michael Scott, with all his sagacity, devise a plan to keep them in innocent employment. He at length discovered one. "Go," says he, "and manufacture me ropes that will carry me to the back of the moon, of those materials, *miller's-sudds* and sea-sand." Michael Scott here obtained rest from his active operators; for, when other work failed them, he always dispatched them to their rope-manufactory. "But," says our relator, "though these agents could never make proper ropes of those materials, their efforts to that effect are far from being contemptible,—for some of their ropes are seen by the seaside till this blessed day."

We shall close our notice of Michael Scott by reciting one anecdote of him in the latter end of his life, which, on that account, will not be the less interesting.

In consequence of a violent quarrel which Michael Scott once had with a person whom he conceived to have caused him some injury, Michael resolved, as the highest punishment he could inflict upon him, to send his adversary to that evil place designed only for Satan and his black companions. He, accordingly, by means of his supernatural machinations, sent the poor unfortunate man thither; and had he been sent by any other means than those of Michael Scott, he would no doubt have met with a warm reception. Out of pure spite to Michael, however, when Satan learned who was his billet-master, he would no more receive him than he would receive the Wife of Beth; and, instead of treating the unfortunate man with that harshness characteristic of him, he showed him considerable civilities. Introducing him to his *"Ben Taigh,"* he directed her to show the stranger any curiosities he might wish to see, hinting very significantly that he had provided some accommodations for their mutual friend Michael Scott, the sight of which might afford him some gratification. The polite housekeeper, accordingly, conducted the stranger through the principal apartments in the house, where he saw sights which, it is hoped, the reader will never witness. But the bed of Michael Scott!—his greatest enemy could not but feel satiate with revenge at the sight of it. It was a place too horrid to be described, filled promiscuously with all the horrid brutes imaginable. Toads and lions, lizards and leeches, and, amongst the rest, not the least conspicuous, a large serpent gaping for Michael Scott, with its mouth wide open. This last sight having satisfied the stranger's curiosity, he was led to the outer gate, and came off with far more agreeable reflections than when he entered.

He reached his friends, and, among other pieces of news touching his travels, he was not backward in relating the entertainment that awaited his friend Michael Scott, as soon as he would *stretch his foot* for the other world. But Michael did not at all appear disconcerted at his friend's intelligence. He affirmed that he would disappoint the d—l and him both in their expectations. In proof of which, he gave the following signs: "When I am just dead," says he, "open my breast, and extract my heart. Carry it to some place where the public may see the result. You will then transfix it upon a long pole, and if Satan will have my soul, he will come in the likeness of a black raven, and carry it off; and if my soul will be saved, it will be carried off by a white dove." His friends faithfully obeyed his instructions. Having exhibited his heart in the manner directed, a large black raven was observed to come from the east with great fleetness; while a white dove came from the west with equal velocity. The raven made a furious dash at the heart, missing which, it was unable to curb its force, till it was considerably past it; and the dove, reaching the spot at the same time, carried off the heart amidst the cheers and ejaculations of the spectators.

CHAPTER IV.
OF THEIR DOMESTIC ECONOMY AND FESTIVE HABITS.

IT is well known that the fairies are a sociable people, passionately given to festive amusements and jocund hilarity. Hence, it seldom happens that they cohabit in pairs, like most other species, but rove about in bands, each band having a stated habitation or residence, to which they resort as occasion suggests.

Their habitations are generally found in rough irregular precipices and broken caverns, remarkable for wildness of scenery, from whence we may infer that they are particularly fond of what we term the Romantic. These habitations are composed of stones, in the form of irregular turrets, of such size and shapes as the nature of the materials and the taste of the architect happened to suggest, and so solid in their structure as frequently to resemble "masses of rocks or earthen hillocks."

Their doors, windows, smoke-vents, and other conveniences, are so artfully constructed, as to be invisible to the naked eye in day-light, though in dark nights splendid lights are frequently reflected through their invisible casements.

Within those "*Tomhans*," or, as others term them, "Shian," sociality and mirth are ever the inmates,—and they are so much addicted to dancing, that it forms their chief and favourite amusement. The length of their reels will be judged of from the following narrative:

"Once upon a time, a tenant in the neighbourhood of Cairngorm in Strathspey emigrated with his family and cattle to the forest of Glenavon, which is well known to be inhabited by many fairies as well as ghosts. Two of his sons having been one night late out in search of some of their sheep which had strayed, they had occasion to pass a fairy turret, or dwelling, of very large dimensions; and what was their astonishment on observing streams of the most refulgent light shining forth through innumerable crevices in the rock—crevices which the sharpest eye in the country had never seen before. Curiosity led them towards the turret, when they were charmed by the most exquisite sounds ever emitted by a fiddle-string, which, joined to the sportive mirth and glee accompanying it, reconciled them in a great measure to the scene, although they knew well enough the inhabitants were fairies. Nay, overpowered by the enchanting jigs played by the fiddler, one of the brothers had even the hardihood to propose that they should pay the occupants of the turret a short visit. To this motion the other brother, fond as he was of dancing, and animated as he was by the music, would by no means consent, and very earnestly inculcated upon his brother many pithy arguments well calculated to restrain his curiosity. But every new jig that was played, and every new reel that was danced, inspired the adventurous brother with additional ardour; and at length, completely fascinated by the enchanting revelry, leaving all prudence behind, at one leap he entered the 'Shian.' The poor forlorn brother was now left in a most uncomfortable situation. His grief for the loss of a brother whom he dearly loved suggested to him more than once the desperate idea of sharing his fate, by following his example. But, on the other hand, when he coolly considered the possibility of sharing very different entertainment from that which rung upon his ears, and remembering, too, the comforts and conveniences of his father's fireside, the idea immediately appeared to him any thing but prudent. After a long and disagreeable altercation between his affection for his brother and his regard for himself, he came to the resolution of trying a middle course;—that is, to send in at the window a few remonstrances to his brother, which if he did not attend to, let the consequences be upon his own head. Accordingly, taking his station at one of the crevices, and calling upon his brother, three several times, by name, as use is, he sent in to him, as aforesaid, the most moving pieces of elocution he could think upon,—imploring him, as he valued his poor parent's life and blessing, to come forth and go home with him, Donald Macgillivray, his thrice affectionate and unhappy brother. But, whether it was he could not hear this eloquent harangue, or, what is more probable, that he did not choose to attend to it, certain it is, that it proved totally ineffectual to accomplish its object,—and the consequence was, that Donald Macgillivray found it equally much his duty and his interest to return home to his family with the melancholy tale of poor Rory's fate. All the prescribed ceremonies calculated to rescue him from the fairy dominion were resorted to by his mourning relatives without effect, and Rory was supposed as lost for ever, when a *wise man* of the day having learned the circumstance, set them upon a plan of having him delivered at the end of twelve months from his entry. 'Return,' says the *Duin Glichd* to Donald, 'to the place where you lost your brother, a year and a day from the time. You will insert in your garment a Rowan Cross, which will protect you from the fairies' interposition. Enter the turret boldly and resolutely, in the name of the Highest claim your brother, and, if he does not accompany you voluntarily, seize him and carry him off by force,—none dare interfere with you.'"

The experiment appeared to the cautious contemplative brother as one that was fraught with no ordinary danger, and he would have most willingly declined the prominent character allotted to him in the performance of it, but for the importunate entreaty of his friends, who implored him, as he valued their blessing, not to slight such excellent advice. Their entreaties, together with his confidence in the virtues of the Rowan Cross, overcame his scruples, and he, at length, agreed to put the experiment in practice, whatever the result might be.

Well then, the important day arrived, when the father of those two sons was destined either to recover his lost son, or to lose the only son he had, and, anxious as the father felt, Donald Macgillivray, the intended adventurer, felt no less on the occasion. The hour of midnight approached, when the drama was to be acted, and Donald Macgillivray, loaded with all the charms and benedictions in his country, took mournful leave of his friends, and proceeded to the scene of his intended enterprise. On approaching the well-known turret, a repetition of that mirth and those ravishing sounds, that had been the source of so much sorrow to himself and family, once more attracted his attention, without at all creating in his mind any extraordinary feelings of satisfaction. On the contrary, he abhorred the sounds most heartily, and felt much greater inclination to recede than to advance. But what was to be done? courage, character, and every thing dear to him, were at stake—so that to advance was his only alternative. In short, he reached the "*Shian*," and after twenty fruitless attempts, he at length entered the place with trembling footsteps, and, amidst the brilliant and jovial scene, the not least gratifying spectacle which presented itself to Donald was his brother Rory earnestly engaged at the Highland Fling on the floor, at which, as might have been expected, he had greatly improved. Without losing much time in satisfying his curiosity, by examining the quality of the company, he ran to his brother, repeating, most vehemently, the words prescribed to him by the "*Wise man*"—seized him by the collar, and insisted he should immediately accompany him home to his poor afflicted parents. Rory assented, provided he would allow him to finish his single reel, assuring Donald, very earnestly, that he had not been half an hour in the house. In vain did the latter assure the former, that, instead of half an hour, he had actually remained twelve months. Nor would he have believed his overjoyed friends on reaching home, "did not the calves, now grown into stots, and the newborn babes, now travelling the house, at length convince him, that in his single reel he had danced for a twelvemonth and a day."

This reel, however, in which Rory Macgillivray had been engaged, although it may be considered of pretty moderate length, will form but a short space in a night's entertainment, of which the following is a brief account:

"Nearly three hundred years ago, there lived in Strathspey two men, greatly celebrated for their performances on the fiddle. It happened upon a certain Christmas time that they had formed the resolution of going to Inverness, to be employed in their musical capacities during that festive season. Accordingly, having arrived in that great town, and secured lodgings, they sent round the newsman and his bell, to announce to the inhabitants their arrival in town, and the object of it, their great celebrity in their own country, the number of tunes they played, and their rate of charge per day, per night, or hour. Very soon after, they were called upon by a venerable-looking old man, grey-haired and somewhat wrinkled, of genteel deportment and liberal disposition; for, instead of grudging their charges, as they expected, he only said that he would double the demand. They cheerfully agreed to accompany him, and soon they found themselves at the door of a very curious dwelling, the appearance of which they did not at all relish. It was night, but still they could easily distinguish the house to be neither like the great Castle Grant, Castle Lethindry, Castle Roy, or Castle-na-muchkeruch at home, nor like any other house they had seen on their travels. It resembled a huge fairy 'Tomhan,' such as are seen in Glenmore. But the mild persuasive eloquence of the guide, reinforced by the irresistible arguments of a purse of gold, soon removed any scruples they felt at the idea of entering so novel a mansion. They entered the place, and all sensations of fear were soon absorbed in those of admiration of the august assembly which surrounded them; strings tuned to sweet harmony soon gave birth to glee in the dwelling. The floor bounded beneath the agile '*fantastic toe*,' and gaiety in its height pervaded every soul present. The night passed on harmoniously, while the diversity of the reels and the loveliness of the dancers presented to the fiddlers the most gratifying scene they ever witnessed; and in the morning, when the ball was terminated, they took their leave, sorry that the time of their engagement was so short, and highly gratified at the liberal treatment which they experienced. But what was their astonishment, on issuing forth from this strange dwelling, when they beheld the novel scene which surrounded them. Instead of coming out of a castle, they found they had come out of a little hill, they knew not what way; and on entering the town they found those objects which yesterday shone in all the splendour of novelty, to-day exhibit only the ruins and ravages of time, while the strange innovations of dress and manners displayed by their numerous spectators filled them with wonder and consternation. At last a mutual understanding took place between themselves and the crowd assembled to look upon them, and a short account of their adventures led the more sagacious part of the spectators to suspect at once that they had been paying a visit to the inhabitants of *Tomnafurich*, which, not long ago, was the grand rendezvous of many of the fairy bands inhabiting the surrounding districts; and the arrival of a very old man on the spot set the matter fairly at rest. On being attracted by the crowd, he walked up to the two poor old oddities, who were the subject of amazement, and having learned their history, thus addressed them: 'You are the two men my great-grandfather lodged, and who, it was supposed, were decoyed by Thomas Rymer to Tomnafurich. Sore did your friends lament your loss—but the lapse of a hundred years has now rendered your name extinct.'

"Finding every circumstance conspire to verify the old man's story, the poor fiddlers were naturally inspired with feelings of reverential awe at the secret wonders of the Deity—and it being the Sabbath-day, they naturally wished to indulge those feelings in a place of worship. They, accordingly, proceeded to church, and took their places, to hear public worship, and sat for a while listening to the pealing bells, which, while they summoned the remainder of the congregation to church, summoned them to their long homes. When the ambassador of peace ascended the sacred place, to announce to his flock the glad tidings of the Gospel—strange to tell, at the first word uttered by his lips, his ancient hearers, the poor deluded fiddlers, both crumbled into dust."

CHAPTER V.
OF THE PASSIONS AND PROPENSITIES OF THE FAIRIES.

THE ingenious reader must not suppose that, because the fairies were once angelic, they have continued so in this corrupt world to the present day. They will be found to exhibit in their conduct as signal proofs of degeneracy from their original innocence and worth as their mortal contemporary, man; and, as may be concluded, this degeneracy has entailed upon them those passions and infirmities, from which they were, no doubt, once on a time exempt.

The fairies are remarkable for the amorousness of their dispositions, and are not very backward in forming attachments and connections with the people that cannot with propriety be called their own species. We are told it is an undeniable fact, that it was once a common practice with both sexes of the fairy people to form intimacies with human swains and damsels, whom they would visit at times and in places highly unbecoming and suspicious; and these improper intimacies not unfrequently produced, as may be well believed, *their natural consequences*. It exposed the fairy-females to that indisposition to which, before their fall, they were no doubt strangers—we mean the pains of child-birth, which, it seems, they suffer in common with their earthly neighbours. To the more sceptical part of our readers, the idea of fairy fruition may appear somewhat incredible. In order, however, to remove any doubt on the subject, we submit the particulars of a fairy accouchement, which took place, no doubt, "a considerable time ago," in the wilds of Cairngorm:

"A considerable time ago there was a woman living in the neighbourhood of Cairngorm in Strathspey, by profession a midwife, of extensive practice, and esteemed, indeed, the best midwife in the district. One night, while she was preparing for bed, there came a loud knocking to her door, indicating great haste in the person that knocked. The midwife was accustomed to such late intrusions, and concluded, even before she opened the door, that her presence was too much required at a *sick-bed*. She found the person that knocked to be a rider and his horse, *both out of breath*, and most impatient for her company. The rider entreated the midwife to make haste, and jump up behind him without a single moment's delay, else that the life of an amiable woman was lost for ever. But the midwife, having a great regard to cleanliness and decorum, requested leave to exchange her apparel before she set out; a motion which, on the part of the rider, was met with a decided negative, and nothing would satisfy the rider but that the midwife would immediately jump up behind him on his grey horse. His importunities were irresistible, the midwife mounted, and off they flew at full gallop. The midwife being now seated, and fleeing on the road, she began naturally to question her guide what he was—where he was going—and how far. He, however, declined immediately making any other reply to her questions than merely saying that she would be well rewarded, which, however consoling, was far from being satisfactory information to the midwife. At length the course they pursued, and the road they took, alarmed the midwife beyond measure, and her guide found it necessary to appease her fears by explaining the matter, otherwise she would, in all probability, prove inadequate to the discharge of her duty. 'My good woman,' says the fairy to the midwife, 'be not alarmed; though I am conducting you to a fairy habitation to assist a fairy lady in distress, be not dismayed, I beseech you; for I promise you, by all that is sacred, you shall sustain no injury, but will be safely restored to your dwelling when your business is effected, with such boon or present as you shall choose to ask or accept of.' The fairy was a sweet good-looking young fellow, and the candour of his speech and the mildness of his demeanour soothed her fears, and reconciled the *Ben Ghlun*, in a great measure, to the enterprise. They were not long in reaching the place, when the midwife found the fairy lady in any thing but easy circumstances, and soon proved the auspicious instrument of bringing to the world a fine lusty boy. All was joy and rejoicing in consequence, and all the fairies in the turret flattered and caressed the midwife. She was desired to choose any gift in the power of fairies to grant, which was instantly to be given her. Upon which she asked, as a boon, that whomsoever she or her posterity should attend in her professional capacity, a safe and speedy delivery should be insured them. The favour was instantly conferred on her, and all know to this day that *Muruch-na-Ban*, the man-midwife, possesses, in no inconsiderable degree, the professional talents of his great-grandmother."

Before concluding this chapter, we owe it, in justice to both the human and fairy communities of the present day, to say, that such intercourse as that described to have taken place betwixt them is now extremely rare; and, with the single exception of a good old shoemaker, now or lately living in the village of Tomantoul, who confesses having had some dalliances with a "*lanan shi*" in his younger days, we do not know personally any one who has carried matters this length.

CHAPTER VI.
OF THE FAIRY'S EMBEZZLING AND CRIMINAL PROPENSITIES.

BUT, although the correspondence now subsisting between the human and fairy people is much more chaste and innocent than it was of old, still it appears that the strong predilection which the fairies entertained for human society is far from being yet extinguished. It is no doubt the existence of this predilection on the part of the former, and the increasing shyness on the part of the latter, that could induce the fairies to resort to those dishonest methods to which they now recur, to have their passion for human society gratified.

We presume the reader is aware that the fairies are much addicted to that heinous crime child-stealing—a crime which these people, in consequence, no doubt, of their long experience in the practice, commit with wonderful address. Often have they robbed the inexperienced mother of her tender babe in the height of day, while his place is taken by an impudent impostor, whose sham sickness and death entail on the unhappy parent an additional load of misery. To warn unsuspicious mothers of the dangers to which themselves and their offspring are exposed from fairy practices, the following narrative may be of use:

"There were once two natives of Strathspey who were in the habit of dealing a little in the whisky way—that is to say, they were accustomed occasionally to visit a family in Glenlivat, from whom they would buy a few barrels, which they would again dispose of among the gentlemen of Badenoch and Fort-William, to pretty good account; and on those occasions, for reasons well known to every district gauger, (an evil death to him!) the Strathspeymen always found it most convenient to travel by night. Well, then, on one of those occasions, as they were busy measuring the whisky in the friend's house at Glenlivat, a little child belonging to the goodman, and which lay in the cradle, uttered a piteous cry, as if it had been shot. The goodwife, according to custom, blessed her child, and, as she supposed, raised it from the cradle. Ascribing the cry merely to infantine frailty or fretfulness, the Strathspeymen took no particular notice of it, and having their business transacted, they proceeded on their way with their cargo. A short distance from their friend's house, they were not a little astonished to find a little child abandoned on the high road, without a being in sight of it. One of the lads took it up in his arms, on which it ceased its plaintive cries, and with great fondness clasped his little hands round his neck, and smiled. This naturally excited some curiosity, and on closer examination they clearly recognised it to be their friend's child. Suspicion was instantly attached to the fairies, and this suspicion was a great deal strengthened by the circumstance of the cry uttered by the child, as already mentioned. Indeed, they came to an immediate conclusion that the fairies, having embezzled the real child, then in their possession, and deposited a stock or substitute in its place, it was the lucky presence of mind discovered by its mother in blessing it, on its having uttered the cry, that rescued it from fairy dominion, for no sooner was the blessing pronounced than they were compelled to abandon the child. As their time was limited, they could not with convenience immediately return to their friend's house to solve the mysterious occurrence, but proceeded on their journey, taking special care of their little foundling.

"In about a fortnight thereafter, having occasion for a few barrels more, they returned to Glenlivat, taking the child along with them, which, however, they concealed on arriving at the father's house. In the course of mutual inquiries for each other's welfare, the goodwife took occasion to lament very bitterly a severe and protracted illness which seized her child on the night of their preceding visit, the nature of which illness could not be ascertained, but, at all events, certain death was the consequence to the child. During this lamentation, the impostor uttered the most piteous cries, and appeared in the last stage of his sufferings; upon this, the lads, without any preliminary remarks, produced their little charge, telling the mother to take courage, that they now presented her with her real child, as healthy and thriving as a trout, and that the object of her great solicitude was nothing more than a barefaced fairy impostor. A short statement of facts induced the happy mother to agree to an exchange, she receiving back her child, and the lads the stock or impostor, to whom his new proprietors proceeded to administer a warm specific commonly given to his kin on similar occasions. They procured an old creel and a bunch of straw, in order to try the effects the burning element would have in curing him of his grievous complaints. But at the appearance of those articles, the stock took the hint, and not choosing to wait a trial of its effects, flew out at the smoke-hole, telling the exulting spectators, on attaining the top of the 'Lum,' that, had it not been for the unfortunate arrival of the two travellers, he should have given the inmates very different entertainment."

When we reflect upon the extreme covetousness manifested by the fairies for human children, the frequent instances of their embezzlement, and, on the other hand, the ease and simplicity by which these robberies can be foiled, we feel persuaded neither mother nor nurse will now neglect the safeguards prescribed for the preservation of children from such practices. It is universally allowed by people conversant in those important matters, that suspending the child's head downwards, on its being dressed in the morning, is an excellent preservative from every species of supernatural agency, and this is certainly a cheap and simple process. A red thread tied about its neck, or a rowan cross, are said to be equally efficacious in preventing the influence of evil spirits, evil eyes, and other calamities of the same description.

But as it is natural to suppose that those precautions will still be sometimes neglected, as they have always too often been, it is fortunate that a remedy has been discovered for those desperate cases, where repentance for past imprudence would not avail. When a child has actually been stolen, and a stock or substitute left in its stead, the child may be recovered in the following manner:—Let the stock be carried to the junction of three shires, or the confluence of three rivers, where it is to be left for the night; and it is a certain fact, that if the child has been stolen by the fairies, they must, in the course of the night, return the genuine offspring, and take away the spurious one.

But children are not the only objects of their envy. They are equally covetous of pregnant females at a certain juncture, when they embrace every opportunity of securing them, well knowing that, by such acquisitions, they obtain a double bargain. The process of stealing women is the same as that of stealing children, only their ranges in quest of such prizes are much more extensive, as the following story will show:

"There was once a courageous clever man, of the name of John Roy, who lived in Glenbrown, in the parish of Abernethy. One night, as John Roy was out traversing the hills for his cattle, he happened to fall in with a fairy banditti, whose manner of travelling indicated that they carried along with them some booty. Recollecting an old, and, it seems, a faithful saying, that the fairies are obliged to exchange any booty they may possess for any return, however unequal in value, on being challenged to that effect, John Roy took off his bonnet, and threw it towards them, demanding a fair exchange in the emphatic Gaelic phrase, *Sluis sho slumus Sheen.* It was, no doubt, an unprofitable barter for the fairies. They, however, it would appear, had no other alternative but to comply with John Roy's demand; and in room of the bonnet, they abandoned the burden, which turned out to be nothing more nor less than a fine fresh lady, who, from her dress and language, appeared to be a *Sasonach.* With great humanity, John Roy conducted the unfortunate lady to his house, where she was treated with the utmost tenderness for several years; and the endearing attentions paid to her by John and his family won so much her affections as to render her soon happy in her lot. Her habits became gradually assimilated to those of her new society; and the Saxon lady was no longer viewed in any other character than as a member of John Roy's family.

"It happened, however, in the course of time, that the *new king* found it necessary to make the great roads through those countries by means of soldiers, for the purpose of letting coaches and carriages pass to the northern cities; and those soldiers had officers and commanders in the same way as our fighting army have now. Those soldiers were never great favourites in these countries, particularly during the time that our own kings were alive; and, consequently, it was no easy matter for them, either officers or men, to procure for themselves comfortable quarters. But John Roy forgot the national animosity of his countrymen to the *Cotton Darg* (red coat), when the latter appealed to his generosity as an individual; and he, accordingly, did not hesitate to offer an asylum under his roof to a *Saxon* captain and his son, who commanded a party employed in his immediate neighbourhood. His offer was thankfully accepted of, and while the strangers were highly delighted at the cleanliness and economy of the house and family of their host, the latter was quite satisfied with the frankness and urbanity of manners displayed by his guests. One thing, however, caused some feelings of uneasiness to John Roy, and that was the extreme curiosity manifested by them, whenever they were in the company or presence of his English foundling, on whom their eyes were continually rivetted, as if she were a ghost or a fairy. On one occasion, it happened that the captain's son lapsed into a state of the profoundest meditation, gazing upon this lady with silent emotion. 'My son,' says the captain, his father, 'tell me what is the cause of your deep meditation?'—'Father,' replies the sweet youth, 'I think on the days that are gone; and of my dearest mother, who is now no more. I have been led into those reflections by the appearance of that lady who is now before me. Oh, father! does she not strikingly resemble the late partner of your heart; she for whom you so often mourn in secret?'—'Indeed, my son,' replied the father, 'the resemblance has frequently recurred to me too forcibly. Never were twin sisters more like; and, were not the thing impossible, I should even say she was my dearest departed wife;'—pronouncing her name as he spoke, and also the names of characters nearly connected to both parties. Attracted by the mention of her real name, which she had not heard repeated for a number of years before, and attracted still more by the nature of their conversation, the lady, on strict examination of the appearance of the strangers, instantly recognised her tender husband and darling son. Natural instinct could be no longer restrained. She threw herself upon her husband's bosom; and Ossian, the son of Fingal, could not describe in adequate terms the transports of joy that prevailed at the meeting. Suffice it to say, that the *Saxon* lady was again restored to her affectionate husband, pure and unblemished as when he lost her, and John Roy gratified by the only reward he would accept of—the pleasure of doing good."

From the sequel of the story, it appears that some of the hordes of fairies, inhabiting the "Shian of Coir-laggack," found it convenient, for purposes which may be easily guessed at, to take a trip to the south of England, and made no scruple to kidnap this lady in the absence of her husband, and on the occasion of her accouchement. A stock was, of course, deposited in her stead—which, of *course*, died in a few days after—and which, of *course*, was interred in the full persuasion of *its* being the lady in question, with all the splendour which her merits deserved. Thus would the perfidious fairies have enjoyed the fruits of their cunning, without even a suspicion of their knavery, were it not for the "cleverness and generosity of John Roy, who once lived in Glenbrown."

The natural passions, lusts, and covetousness of which we have now shown the fairies to be possessed, are not, however, our only grounds for calling in question the fitness of their title to angelic nature and attributes. For it will be seen, from some traits in their character about to be detailed, that their appetites are as keen and voluptuous as their inclinations are corrupt and wicked. Our readers would be apt to believe, from the first outline of their character, that they were an amiable, harmless race of people, strictly honest, and given entirely to innocent amusements. But it is a fact too well known, that many of them are employed in very different avocations from mirth and dancing; for, to repeat an old Scottish proverb, "if a' tales be true," thieving and blackguarding occupy fully as much of their time as mirth and dancing. And what is still worse, it is much suspected that their proneness to theft and knavery is not so much the effect of necessity, as it is the effect of wanton depravity. However base and degrading in the eyes of society appears the thief, even when his deviation from honesty is the result of *sheer* necessity, he appears infinitely more so when he is solely led to the commission of crimes from wanton levity. Hence the indignation which a worthy man feels, whenever those pilfering depredators embezzle the fruits of his honest industry. The *whirlwind* is not the alone engine of robbery to which the fairies resort; they recur to others of a more direct and ruinous character; while the loser, from the speciousness of their artifices, is seldom conscious of the true cause of his loss. In order to expose the wantonness of such pillage as they will be shown to be guilty of, we need only call our reader's attention to the extent of the indisputable perquisites which they derive from fire and other calamities incident to the estate of man, many of which calamities, we are told, are accomplished by their agency. As, however, we would not readily accuse them of crimes so atrocious, without some foundation, we submit the following particulars to the judgment of our readers, leaving them to draw their own inferences.

"One day a fairy woman, residing in the turrets of Craig-Aulnaic, called on one of the tenants' wives in Delnabo, in her neighbourhood, and requested of her the loan of a firlot of oatmeal for meat to her family, promising she would return it in a very short time, as she herself hourly expected a considerable supply. Not choosing, for so small a trifle, to incur the fairy's displeasure, the tenant's wife complied with her request, from the same motives as if she had been the exciseman. After regaling the fairy with a dram and bread and cheese, as is the custom of the country, she went out to give her the customary convoy. On ascending the eminence above the town, the '*Benshi*' paused, and, with apparent exultation, told the tenant's wife that she might take her meal home with her, as she herself was now supplied as she expected. The woman, without putting any impertinent questions to the lady as to the source whence her supply proceeded, cheerfully agreed to receive back her meal, and took leave of her visitor. She was not a little surprised, however, to observe, in a few minutes thereafter, the corn-kiln of an adjacent farm in total conflagration, with all its contents."

Over and above this, all liquids spilled on the ground are supposed to go to their use; and there are some people even so charitable as purposely to reserve for their participation a share of the best they possess. It is not unlikely that such generous actions were in some degree influenced by such returns as the following:—

"Once upon a time, a farmer, in Strathspey, was engaged sowing a field upon his farm, and, as is not uncommon, he accompanied his labours with a cheerful song. Now the fairies are very fond of music, and not less so of spoil,—and whether it was the music or the seed that attracted her most to the spot, certain it is, that a fairy damsel, of great beauty and elegance, presented herself to the farmer. She requested of him, as a particular favour, to sing her an old Gaelic song, '*Nighan Donne na Bual*,' and, when this favour was granted her, she sought of him a present of corn. Although he had far less objections to her first request than he had to her second, he did not flatly refuse her, but he did what any prudent man would do in similar circumstances,—he inquired what she would give him in return. She answered, that, provided he granted her request, his seed would not the more speedily fail him; and this assurance she enforced with a look so significant, as to induce him at once to supply her very liberally from his bag. She then departed, and he resumed his work. He was soon after very agreeably surprised, when he found that, after sowing abundantly a large field, wont to take five times the bulk of his bag, it appeared equal in size and weight to what it was when he met with the fairy nymph. Far from being in the least confounded at the agreeable circumstance, he threw his bag over his shoulder, highly satisfied at the act of munificence he did in the morning, and sowed with it another field of equal extent, without its exhibiting any appearance of diminution. Perfectly satisfied now with his day's labour, he returned home, fully determined to take care of his bag. But, just as he was entering the barn door, who met him but his wife, 'who was a foolish talkative hussey, having a tongue as long, and a head as empty, as the parish church bell.' With her usual loquacity she accosted him, expressing her astonishment at the unaccountable nature of the sack, that had thus sown half their farm,—expressing, moreover, very notable suspicions of the cause. Now it is well known that, whenever any supernatural agency is challenged, the spell is instantly broken. So that the clashmaclavering Jezebel had scarcely uttered those inconsiderate and highly reprehensible words, when the burden on the farmer's back became an empty bag. 'I'll be your death, you foolish, foolish woman,' exclaimed her woe-struck husband; 'were it not for your imprudent talk, this bag were worth its weight of gold.'"

Such relations as the foregoing should go very far to induce every prudent and foreseeing man to be on as friendly a footing as possible with those capricious and all-powerful people, especially when their friendship is to be purchased on such reasonable terms as those of which we have just read. The unhappy hero of the following narrative was convinced, when too late, of the truth of this observation.

"A farmer, who at one time occupied the farm of Auchriachan, of Strathavon, was one day searching for his goats in a remote hill in Glenlivat, and what came on but a thick hazy fog, which marred his way, and bewildered his senses. Every stone, magnified by the delusion of the moment, appeared a mountain; every rivulet seemed to him to run in an opposite direction to its usual course; and the unhappy traveller thought of his fireside, which he expected never to see more. Night came on apace; its horrific gloom, as it approached, dispelled the unhappy wanderer's forlorn hopes, and he now sat down to prepare for the world that has no end. Involved in perplexity at his unhappy situation, he threw a mournful look on the gloomy scene around him, as if to bid the world an eternal adieu,— when, lo! a twinkling light glimmered on his eye. It was a cheering blink that administered comfort to his soul. His frigid limbs, which lately refused their office, recovered their vigour. His exhausted frame became animated and energetic; and he immediately directed his course towards the light, which, from its reflection, seemed not far distant. On reaching the place, however, his joy was a good deal damped when he examined the nature of the place whence the light reflected. A human foot never seemed to have visited the scene; it was one of wildness and horror. Life, however, is exceedingly sweet when we are on the brink of losing it, and necessity had so far subdued every vestige of fear, that *Auchriachan* resolved at all hazards to take a night's lodging with the inmates, whatever their nature or calling might be. The door was open, and he entered the place. His courage, however, was a good deal appalled, on meeting at the door an old female acquaintance, whose funeral he had recently attended, and who, it appeared, acted in this family in the capacity of housewife. But this meeting, however disagreeable it proved to Auchriachan in one respect, ultimately turned out a fortunate circumstance for him, inasmuch as his old acquaintance was the happy means of saving his life. On observing Auchriachan—for that was the farmer's title—enter the abode, she instantly ran towards him, and told him he was done for, unless he chose to slip in into a bye-corner off the principal apartment, where he had better remain until she found an opportunity of effecting his escape. The advice of the friendly housekeeper he thought it prudent to adopt, and he was accordingly content to hide himself in a crevice in the apartment. Scarce had he done so, when there entered the dwelling an immense concourse of fairies, who had been all day absent upon some important expedition; and being well appetized by their journey, they all cried out for some food. Having all sat in council, the question proposed for discussion was, 'What was their supper to consist of?'—When an old sagacious looking fairy, who sat in the chimney corner, spoke as follows: 'Celestial gentlemen, you all know and abhor that old miserly fellow the taxman of Auchriachan. Mean and penurious, he appropriates nothing to us; but, on the contrary, disappoints us of our very dues. By learning too well the lesson taught him by his old and wizened grand-mother, nothing escapes a blessing and a safeguard; and the consequence is, that we cannot interfere with the gleanings on his fields, far less the stock and produce. Now, Auchriachan himself is not at home this night; he is in search of his goats, our allies,— his less careful household have neglected the customary safeguards; and, lo! his goods are at our mercy. Come, let us have his favourite ox to supper.'— 'Bravo!' exclaimed the whole assembly; 'the opinion of Thomas Rymer is always judicious; Auchriachan is certainly a miserable devil, and we shall have his favourite ox to supper.'—'But whence shall we procure bread to eat with him?' inquired a greedy-looking fairy. 'We shall have the new baken bread of Auchriachan,' replied the sagacious and sage counsellor, Mr. Rymer; 'for he is a miserly old fellow—he himself is not at home, and his wife has forgot to cross the first bannock.'—'Bravo!' exclaimed the whole assembly. 'By all means, let us have the new baken bread of Auchriachan.'

"Thus did Auchriachan, honest man, who, indeed, was not at home, with no very grateful feelings, learn the fate of his favourite ox, without, however, dissenting from the general voice that pronounced his doom. And, in pursuance of the same unpleasant decision, he had the additional mortification to see his ill-fated ox deliberately introduced by the nose and killed in his presence. Meantime, when all were engaged cooking the ox, the officious housekeeper took occasion, under pretence of some other errand, to relieve Auchriachan from his uncomfortable seclusion. On issuing forth from Mr. Rymer's council-chamber, Auchriachan found the mist had entirely disappeared—the stones were now of their natural size—the rivulets now ran their usual course—the moon threw her silver mantle over the lately murky scene, and he had now no difficulty to make his way home, lamenting most sincerely the lot of his favourite ox.

"On arriving at home, he was cordially welcomed by his happy family, whose great anxiety for his safety was probably the cause of the omission of that duty that poor Auchriachan had so much cause to deplore. His overjoyed wife, supposing her husband to be no doubt in a hungry case, provided a basket of new baked bread and milk, and urged him to eat, for sure he might well be hungry. He did not, however, mind her solicitude for his comfort—he was sorry and sullen, and cared not for the provision, particularly the bread, well knowing it was only an abominable phantom. At last he inquired, 'Which of you served the oxen this night, my lads?'—'It was I, my father,' replied one of his sons. 'And did you mind the customary safeguard?'—'Indeed,' says the son, 'from my great agitation for the fate of my father, I believe I forgot.'—'Alas! alas!' exclaimed the affectionate farmer, 'my dear and favourite ox is no more!'—'What!' exclaims one of his sons, 'I saw him alive not two hours ago!'—'It was only a fairy stock,' says Auchriachan. 'Bring him out here until I dispatch him.' The farmer then, venting the most unqualified expressions of his indignation upon the stock and its knavish proprietors, struck it such a pithy blow on the forehead as felled it to the ground. Rolling down the brae, at the back of the house, to the bottom, there it lay and the bread along with it, both unmolested; for it was a remarkable circumstance, that neither dog nor cat ever put a tooth on the carcase."

It now only remains for us to describe the most heinous of all their crimes, a crime which we are peculiarly reluctant to bring so openly to light, did not our impartiality as an historian compel us. This crime consists in their destruction of human beings, and their cattle, by means of their magical dart, commonly called an elf-bolt. Those bolts are of various sizes, of a hard yellowish substance, resembling somewhat the flint, for which they are no bad substitutes. The bolt is very frequently of the shape of a heart, its edges being indented like a saw, and very sharp at the point. This deadly weapon the wicked fairy will throw at man or beast with such precision as seldom to miss his aim; and whenever it hits, the stroke is fatal. Such is the great force with which it is flung, that on its striking the object it instantaneously perforates it to the heart, and a sudden death is the consequence. In the blinking of an eye, a man or an ox is struck down cold-dead, and, strange to say, the wound is not discernible to an ordinary person, unless he is possessed of the charm that enables some wise people to trace the course of the bolt, and ultimately discover it in the dead body.—Note, whenever this fatal instrument is discovered, it should be carefully preserved, as it defends its possessor from the fatal consequences of the "*Fay*," so long as he retains it about him.

Having now travelled over the leading traits of the fairy's character, publicly and privately, we shall now conclude our treatise of him by subjoining a few of the most approved cures and safeguards, which afford protection from his dangerous practices. An abler historian might be disposed to offer some learned observations on the strange incongruity of character exhibited by the fairy in the preceding sketches, and endeavour, if he could, to reconcile them so as to form any thing like a rational subject. As a plain unvarnished compiler, however, we have discharged our duty; we have detailed, to the best of our ability, the fairy's character, according to the nature of our materials; and if our delineations are strange and inconsistent, the fault lies either with the fairy or his professed historians, and not with the mere machine, *ourself*, the compiler.

Go to the summit of some stupendous cliff or mountain, where any species of quadruped has never fed nor trod, and gather of that herb in the Gaelic language called "*Mohan*," which can be pointed out by any "*wise* person." This herb you will give to a cow, and of the milk of that cow you are to make a cheese, and whoever eats of that cheese is for ever after, as well as his gear, perfectly secure from every species of fairy agency.

A piece of torch fir carried about the person, and a knife made of iron which has never been applied to any purpose, are both excellent preservatives.

A piece of cold iron or steel put into the bed of a lady "*uneasy in her circumstances*" will protect mother and offspring from being "*Fayed*."

PART III.

Brownies.
Brownie has got a cowl and coat,
And never more will work a jot.

BROWNIES.

ALTHOUGH this mysterious and very useful agent has now become very rare among the Highland mountains, it appears that, at one time, he was the common appendage of every family of rank in those countries. Hence, his history and character are well known; and his memory still retains a powerful interest in the minds of the inhabitants. It may not, therefore, be improper to give a condensed account of the most prominent traits of the Highland Brownie's character, to enable the reader to compare his manners and habits with those of the Brownie of Bodspeck, or any other Brownie with the manners of whom he may happen to be acquainted.

With regard to the Brownie's origin, it is a point that is involved in much obscurity. It was always a peculiar trait in his character, that he never would favour his earthly acquaintances with any information regarding his own private affairs. From some resemblance the Brownie bore to the Fairy, joined to a similarity of habits, it was shrewdly suspected by the more discriminating sort of people, that if he were not actually a member of the Fairy people, he was, at least, a mongrel species of them. But on this important topic the sagacious Brownie himself opened not his mouth; leaving them to argue the matter as they thought proper.

In his personal appearance, the Highland Brownie was highly interesting. His person was not quite so tall as that of the Fairy, but it was well proportioned and comely; and, from the peculiar brownness of his complexion, he received the appellation of *Brownie*.

In his manners and habits he differed widely from all the supernatural beings of his day; inasmuch as he was laborious and faithful to his master's interest—content to labour day and night for no other fee or reward than a scanty diet, and occasionally a suit of cast-off apparel. Hence, the possession of so cheap and useful an agent was an acquisition highly desirable. But he was what neither money nor interest could procure. Having once united himself to the founder of an ancient family, he adhered to him and to his issue so long as he had any lineal posterity; and hence it is, that the Brownie was only found the heir-loom of an ancient and honourable family.

Unexampled for his fidelity, he was the indefatigable guardian and promoter of his adopted master's interest; and, from his powers of prophecy and information, his services were truly invaluable. Over the servants he was always a vigilant and faithful spy, ready to give a faithful account of their good or bad actions; and hence it followed, that with these he was very seldom on a good understanding. So that, if the Brownie was left to the servants' mercy, he would not, in all likelihood, fare the better for his fidelity. But if the master had any regard to his own interest, he was careful to have seen him properly cared for in his meat and in his drink, which care was rewarded by the most unlimited devotion to his interest.

The last two brownies known in this quarter of the Highlands were long the appendages of the ancient family of Tullochgorm in Strathspey. They were male and female, and, for aught we know, they might likewise have been man and wife. The male was of an exceedingly jocose and humorous disposition, often indulging in little sports at the expense of his fellow-servants. He had, in particular, a great trick of flinging clods at the passengers, and from thence he got the name of "*Brownie-Clod.*" He had, however, with all his humour, a great deal of simplicity about him, and became, in his turn, the dupe of those on whom he affected to play. An eminent instance of this appears from a contract into which he foolishly entered with the servants of Tullochgorm, whereby he bound and obliged himself to thrash as much corn and straw as two men could do for the space of a whole winter, on condition he was to be gratified with an old coat and a Kilmarnock cowl, pieces of apparel for which, it seems, he had a great liking. While the servants were reclining themselves at their ease upon the straw, poor Brownie-Clod thrashed on unremittingly, and performed such Herculean tasks as no human constitution could bear for a week together. Some time before the expiry of the contract, the lads, out of pure gratitude and pity, left the coat and cowl for him on a mow of corn in the barn, on receipt of which he instantly struck work, and with the greatest triumph at the idea of taking in his acquaintances, he sneeringly told them, that, since they were so foolish as to give him the coat and cowl before he had wrought for them, he would now decline to thrash another sheaf.

"Huar Prownie coad agus curochd

Agus cha dian Prownie opar tullidh."

The female was more pawky in her ways; and, instead of being a laughing-stock to the female-servants with whom she wrought, she was a sort of a mistress over them. She was seldom on good terms with them, in consequence of the fidelity with which she reported their neglect of duty to their master or mistress. It was her custom to wear a superabundance of hair, in consequence of which, she was commonly called "*Maug Vuluchd,*" or "Hairy Mag." Mag was an honest and excellent housekeeper, and had the service of the table generally assigned her, in which capacity she was extremely useful. The dexterity and care with which she covered the table, always invisible, was not less amusing to strangers than it was convenient to their host. Whatever was called for came as if it floated on the air, and lighted on the table with the utmost ease and celerity; and, for cleanliness and attention, she had not her equal in this land.

PART IV.
Water-Kelpies.

When thaws dissolve the snawy hoord,

An' float the jingling icy boord,

The water-kelpies haunt the foord,

By your direction,

And nightly travellers are allur'd

To their destruction.

BURNS' *Address to the Deil.*

WATER-KELPIES.

IN the former and darker ages of the world when people had not half the wit and sagacity they now possess, and when, consequently, they were much easier duped by such designing agents, the "Ech Uisque," or *Water-Horse*, as the Kelpie is commonly called, was a well-known character in those countries. The Kelpie was an infernal agent, retained in the service and pay of Satan, who granted him a commission to execute such services as appeared profitable to his interest. He was an amphibious character, and generally took up his residence in lochs and pools, bordering on public roads and other situations, most convenient for his professional calling.

His commission consisted in the destruction of human beings, without affording them time to prepare for their immortal interests, and thus endeavour to send their souls to his master, while he, the Kelpie, enjoyed the body. However, he had no authority to touch a human being of his own free accord, unless the latter was the aggressor. In order, therefore, to delude public travellers and others to their destruction, it was the common practice of the Kelpie to assume the most fascinating form, and assimilate himself to that likeness which he supposed most congenial to the inclinations of his intended victim. The likeness of a fine riding steed was his favourite disguise. Decked out in the most splendid riding accoutrements, the perfidious Kelpie would place himself in the weary traveller's way, and graze by the road-side with all the seeming innocence and simplicity in the world. The traveller, supposing this fine horse to have strayed from his master, and considering him as a good *catch* for carrying him a part of the way, would approach the horse with the greatest caution, soothing it with *proogy proogy*, and many other terms of endearment, in the event of his taking to his heels, as wild horses are sometimes apt to do. But this horse knew better what he was about; he was as calm and peaceable as a lamb, until his victim was once fairly mounted on his back; with a fiend-like yell he would then announce his triumph, and plunging headlong with his woe-struck rider into an adjacent pool, enjoy him for his repast. The following curious relation, communicated to the compiler by the celebrated Mr. Wellox, who possesses the precious relic captured from the kelpie alluded to in the story, will complete all the information that is necessary regarding this once formidable entrapper of mankind:

"In the time of my renowned ancestor, Mr. James Macgrigor, (rest to his soul!) who was well known to be a good man, and a man of great strength and courage in his day, there was a most mischievous water-kelpie that lived in Lochness, and which committed the most atrocious excesses on the defenceless inhabitants of the surrounding districts. It was the common practice of this iniquitous agent to prowl about the public roads, decked out in all the trappings of a riding horse, and in this disguise place himself in the way of the passenger, who often took it into his head to mount him, to his no small prejudice; for upon this the vicious brute would immediately fly into the air, and in a jiffy light with his rider in Lochnadorb, Lochspynie, or Lochness, where he would enjoy his victim at his leisure. Filled with indignation at the repeated relations he had heard of the kelpie's practices, my ancestor, Mr. Macgrigor, ardently wished to fall in with his kelpieship, in order to have a bit of a communing with him touching his notorious practices. And Providence, in its wise economy, thought it meet that Mr. Macgrigor should be gratified in his wish.

"One day as he was travelling along '*Slochd Muichd*,' a wild and solitary pass on the road between Strathspey and Inverness, whom did he observe but this identical water-kelpie, browsing away by the road-side with the greatest complacency, thinking, no doubt, in his mind, that he would kidnap Mr. Macgrigor as he had done others. But in this idea he found himself wofully mistaken! For no sooner did Mr. Macgrigor espy him, than he instantly determined to have a trial of his mettle. Accordingly, marching up to the horse, who thought, no doubt, he was just coming to mount him, Mr. Macgrigor soon convinced him of the contrary by drawing his trusty sword, with which he dealt the kelpie such a pithy blow on the nose, as almost felled him to the ground. The stroke maltreated the kelpie's jaw very considerably, cutting through his bridle, in consequence of which, one of the bits, being that which you have just examined, fell down on the ground. Observing the bit lying at his feet, Mr. Macgrigor had the curiosity to pick it up, whilst the astonished kelpie was recovering from the effects of the blow, and this bit Mr. Macgrigor carelessly threw into his pocket. He then prepared for a renewal of his conflict with its former owner, naturally supposing the kelpie would return him his compliment. But what was Mr. Macgrigor's surprise, when he found that, instead of retorting his blow, and fighting out the matter to the last, the kelpie commenced a cool dissertation upon the injustice and illegality of Mr. Macgrigor's proceedings. 'What is your business with me?' says he. 'What is your business with me, Mr. Macgrigor? I have often heard of you as a man of great honour and humanity; why, therefore, thus abuse a poor defenceless animal like me, let me be a horse, or let me be a kelpie, so long as I did you no harm? In my humble opinion, Mr. Macgrigor,' continued the kelpie, 'you acted both cruelly and illegally; and certainly your conduct would justify me, if I should return you twofold your assault upon me. However, I abominate quarrels of this sort,' says the conciliatory kelpie, 'and if you peaceably return me the bit of my bridle, we shall say no more on the subject.' To this learned argument of the kelpie Mr. Macgrigor made no other reply than flatly denying his request, in the first place; and, in the second place, mentioning, in pretty unqualified terms, his opinion of his character and profession. 'It is true,' replied the other, 'that I am what you call a kelpie; but it is known to my heart, that my profession was never quite congenial to my feelings. We kelpies engage in many *disagreeable undertakings*. But, as the proverb says, Necessity has no law; and there is no profession that a man or spirit will not sometimes try, *for the sake of an honest livelihood*: so you will please have the goodness to give me the bit of my bridle.' Observing the great anxiety evinced by the kelpie to have the bit of his bridle restored to him, and feeling anxious to learn its properties, my sagacious ancestor immediately concocted a plan, whereby he might elicit from the poor dupe of a kelpie an account of its virtues. 'Well, Mr. Kelpie,' says Mr. Macgrigor, 'all your logic cannot change my opinion of the criminality of your profession, though, I confess, it has somewhat disarmed me of my personal hostility to you as a member of it; I am, therefore, disposed to deliver up to you the bit of your bridle, but it is on this express condition, that you will favour me with an account of its use and qualities, for I am naturally very *curious*, do you know.' To this proposition the kelpie joyfully acceded, and thus addressed Mr. Macgrigor: 'My dear sir, you must know that such agents as I are invested by our Royal Master with a particular commission, consisting of some document delivered to us by his own hand. The commission delivered to a kelpie consists in a bridle invested with all those powers of transformation, information, and observation, necessary for our calling; and wherever we lose this commission, whether voluntarily or by accident, our power is at an end, and certain annihilation within four and twenty hours is the consequence. Had it not been that my bridle was broken by your matchless blow, I must be so candid as to declare, I might have broken every bone in your body; but now you are stronger than myself, and you can be half a kelpie at your pleasure: only please to look through the holes of the bit of the bridle, and you will see myriads of invisible agents, fairies, witches, and devils, all flying around you, the same as if you had been gifted with the second-sight, and all their machinations clearly exposed to your observation.'—'My dear sir,' replied my ancestor, 'I am much obliged to you for your information; but I am sorry to inform you, that your relation has so endeared the bit of your bridle to myself, that I have resolved to keep it for your sake. I could not persuade myself to part with it for any consideration whatever.'—'What!' exclaimed the petrified Kelpie, 'do you really mean, in the face of our solemn agreement, to retain the bit of my bridle?'—'I not only mean it, but I am resolved on it,' replies my ancestor, who immediately proceeded to make the best of his way home with the bit. 'Come, come,' the Kelpie would perpetually exclaim, 'you have carried the joke far enough, you surely do not mean to keep my bridle?'—'Time will show,' was always his laconic answer. The Kelpie still continued his earnest entreaties, interlarded with anecdotes of great squabbles which he had formerly had with as powerful characters as Mr. Macgrigor, and which always ended to his eminent advantage, but which, he politely insinuated, he would be sorry to see repeated. But when his grief and solicitude for his bridle began to evince themselves in a threatening aspect, a single flourish of his trusty sword disarmed him of all his might, and made him calm as a cat. At length, when they arrived in sight of Mr. Macgrigor's house, his grief and despair for his bridle became perfectly outrageous. Galloping off before Mr. Macgrigor, the Kelpie told him as he went, that he and the bit should never pass his threshold together; and, in pursuance of this assurance, he planted himself in Mr. Macgrigor's door, summoning up all his powers for the impending conflict. However, James Macgrigor resolved, if possible, to evade the Kelpie's decree; and accordingly going to a back window in his house, he called his wife towards him, and threw the bit of the Kelpie's bridle into her lap. He then returned to the Kelpie, who stood sentry at his door, and told him candidly he was a miserable legislator; for that, in spite of his decree, the bit of his bridle was that moment in his wife's possession. The Kelpie, now finding himself fairly outwitted, saw the vanity of contending with James Macgrigor and his claymore, for what could not be recovered. As there was a rowan cross above the door, his kelpieship could no more enter the house than he could pass through the eye of a needle; and he, therefore, thought it best to take himself off, holding forth, at the same time, the most beastly language to my ancestor, which he most sincerely despised."

PART V.
Spunkies.

An' oft your moss-traversing spunkies
Decoy some wight that late and drunk is;
The bleezin, curst, mischievous monkies
Delude his eyes,
Till in some miry slough he sunk is,
Ne'er more to rise.

BURNS' *Address to the Deil.*

SPUNKIES.

THE Spunkie is another of those now-retired ministers, formerly employed by the Enemy of mankind to accomplish their destruction. And, in all truth, he could not have taken into his pay a servant more faithful to his trust than the spunkie. Whenever the traveller had the misfortune to lose his way, or whenever there was a prospect of deluding him from it, this vigilant *link-boy* was ever at hand, to light him into far worse quarters than even the purlieus of Covent Garden.

Suddenly the traveller's attention was arrested by the most resplendent light, apparently reflected from a window not far distant; which, however, as the traveller approached, receded from him like the rainbow. Still pursuing his course towards it, the wily spunkie manœuvred so dexterously, that the unhappy wanderer was speedily decoyed into the nearest moss or precipice. Plunging headlong into some fatal abyss, the deluded victim never returned to his mourning wife and family, to relate to them the spunkie's perfidy.

Happily now, however, the roads are better, and travellers more cautious. All the glittering meteors of the spunkie cannot make the knowing Highlander of the present day turn to the right or to the left. So that the spunkie has now shut shop, and become bankrupt in his department.

PART VI.
Witchcraft.

When Satan, for weighty dispatches,

Sought messengers cunning and bold,

He pass'd by the beautiful faces,

And pick'd out the ugly and old.

VOLLE.

CHAPTER I.
ORIGIN AND HISTORY OF WITCHCRAFT.

WE are now come to consider and describe the ancient and well-known order of Witchcraft; the nature and object of which require very little explanation in a country where it has been so long established as in Scotland. Taking a retrospective view of the rise and progress of this once flourishing institution, we are told it was founded by the Grand Master, shortly after the creation of the world. That the wickedness of the inhabitants having kept pace with their increase, Satan found work multiplying so fast on his hands, that his own spiritual minions, numerous as they were, became inadequate to their employment. Being seldom blind to his own interest, the idea of enlisting a few human instruments to supply their deficiencies naturally suggested itself to his fertile genius, and such has been the thirst for magic and power, which has at all times pervaded the old women of those countries, that he never had great difficulty in procuring abundance of volunteers to join his banners.

Having thus established his new order of emissaries, Satan found them to answer his purposes uncommonly well. They drudged on in his work so laboriously, and with such good success, that he found them more profitable tools, for deluding and *hooking-in* the best portion of mankind, than his own proper agents, whose means of communication and seduction were much more confined and disadvantageous. Accordingly, he has found it his interest to continue the institution to this day.

It will, no doubt, prove a matter of some astonishment to the amiable and considerate reader, how any body that has the honour of wearing a human face could think of espousing so desperate a cause, for the sake of any gratification which Satan's kingdom affords. Common fame errs too much, if he is at all a liberal master to those who are his servants, for it is said he seldom or never fulfils his conditions with any one of them. Though mighty forward to enter into pactions, and extraordinarily liberal in his terms while making a bargain, he is said to be far less ready to perform his share of the conditions when it is once concluded; and what is still worse, when he forfeits a penalty, there is no law that can exact it of him. Accordingly, we have heard of not a few deluded mortals, who sold themselves to him for sums of money and other considerations, but never yet heard of his having paid the purchase money.

So once fared a poor needy wretch of a Highlandman, that bartered his soul to Satan for a cow, and who never could get the latter to fulfil his bargain. It is no doubt true, that after much importunity he did at length perform his stipulation, in a way not very creditable to him. Urgently importuned by the disponer to give him his cow, he ultimately fetched him one, which was but a few hours in his possession, when it was challenged by a third party as his stolen property; unwilling to explain how he came by it, the poor fellow was flung into a prison, and speedily brought before the laird for trial. In this distressing situation, the disponer was compelled to tell the truth and the manner he came by the cow, not doubting but that the disclosure would have at once exculpated him from the charge. But unfortunately for him, his ingenuous confession failed of its object, and the poor man was condemned to the *wuddie*, reserving to him such recourse against Satan as he might be advised to adopt.

CHAPTER II.
OF THE AGENT'S QUALIFICATIONS, AND CEREMONIES OF THEIR CONSTITUTION.

WHEN the candidates for Satan's employment have, by a course of probation, given sufficient proofs of their ability for the discharge of the duties of the profession they are about to adopt, and when they have arrived at an age befitting the importance of the calling, men and women are equally eligible, though it is well known that women are preferred. Their initiation into infernal orders is preceded by the execution of a formal covenant with Satan, sealed with the mutual blood of the parties, whereby, for the considerations therein expressed, Satan engages, on the one hand, to commit to the entrant the various powers and qualifications which shall be detailed in the following pages; and, on the other hand, the said entrant binds and obliges himself, or herself, to apply himself, or herself, faithfully and diligently in his service, by day and by night, promising to conceal the secrets of his trade and profession, (much in the style of our common indentures). The candidates are then inducted into the mysteries and secrets of their new profession with great pomp, in presence of the Royal Grand Master, who, set forth in *proprio terrore*, presides over the ceremony. The place selected for this imposing ceremony is not unfrequently a spacious lake or pool, the members of the craft in attendance being furnished with their seaworthy navy, their brooms and riddles. The following particulars relative to an intended initiation, which was attempted in Strathdown, "in the memory of the grandmothers of some people still living," while it conveys some idea of such a scene as that to which we alluded, may also prove a warning to those who may be thoughtlessly led to embrace the profession.

"In the time of my grandmother, the farm of *Delnabo* was proportionally divided between three tenants. At first equally comfortable in their circumstances, it was in the course of some time remarked by all, and by none more forcibly than by one of the said three portioners, that, although superior in point of industry and talent to his two fellow-portioners, one of the tenants was daily lapsing into poverty, while his two neighbours were daily improving in estate. Amazed and grieved at the adverse fortune which thus attended his family, compared to the prosperous condition of his neighbours, the wife of the poor man was in the habit of expressing her astonishment at the circumstance, not only to her own particular friends, but likewise to the wives of her neighbours themselves. On one of these occasions, the other two wives asked her what would she do to ameliorate her condition, if it were in her power? She answered them, she would do any thing whatever. (Here the other wives thought they had got a gudgeon, that would snap at any bait, and immediately resolved to make her their confidant.) 'Well, then,' says one of the other two wives, 'if you agree to keep our communications strictly secret, and implicitly obey our instructions, neither poverty nor want shall ever assail you more.' This speech of the other wife immediately impressed the poor man's wife with a strong suspicion of their real character. Dissembling all surprise at the circumstance, she promised to agree to all their conditions. She was then directed, when she went to bed that night, to carry along with her the floor-broom, well known for its magical properties, which she was to leave by her husband's side in the course of the night, and which would represent her so exactly, that the husband could not distinguish the difference in the morning. They, at the same time, enjoined her to discard all fears of detection, as their own husbands had been satisfied with those lovely substitutes (the brooms) for a great number of years. Matters being thus arranged, she was desired to join them at the hour of midnight, in order to accompany them to that scene which was to realize her future happiness.

"Promising to attend to their instructions, the poor man's wife took leave of her neighbours, full of those sensations of horror which the discovery of such depravity was calculated to produce in a virtuous mind. Hastening home to her husband, she thought it no crime to break her promise to her wicked neighbours, and, like a dutiful and prudent wife, to reveal to the husband of her bosom the whole particulars of their interview. The husband greatly commended his wife's fidelity, and immediately entered into a collusion with her, which displays no ordinary degree of ingenuity. It was agreed that the husband should exchange apparel with the wife, and that he should, in this disguise, accompany the wives to the place appointed, to see what cantrips they intended to perform. He accordingly arrayed himself in his wife's habiliments, and, at the hour of midnight, joined the party at the place appointed. The '*Bride*,' as they called him, was most cordially received by the two Ladies of the Broom, who warmly congratulated the 'Bride' upon *her* good fortune, and the speedy consummation of *her* happiness. He was then presented with a fir-torch, a broom, and a riddle, articles with which they themselves were furnished. They directed their course along the banks of the rolling Avon, until they reached Craic-pol-nain, or the Craig of the Birdspool. Here, in consequence of the steepness of the craig, they found it convenient to pass to the other side of the river. This passage they effected without the use of their navy, the river being fordable at the place. They then came in sight of Pol-nain, and, lo! what human eye ever witnessed such a scene before! The pool appeared as if actually enveloped in a flame of fire. A hundred torches blazed aloft, reflecting their beams on the towering woods of Loynchork.

And what ear ever heard such shrieks and yells as proceeded from the horrid crew engaged at their hellish orgies on Pol-nain? Those cries were, however, sweet music to the two wives of Delnabo. Every yell produced from them a burst of unrestrained pleasure, and away they frisked, leaving the amiable *bride* a considerable way behind. For the fact is, that he was in no hurry to reach the scene, and when he did reach it, it was with a determination to be only a spectator, and not a participator in the night's performance. On reaching the pool's side he saw what was going on,—he saw abundance of hags steering themselves to and fro in their riddles, by means of their oars the brooms, hallooing and skirling worse than the bogles, and each holding in her left hand a torch of fir,—whilst at other times they would swirl themselves into a row, and make profound obeisance to a large black ugly tyke, perched on a lofty rock, who was no doubt the 'muckle thief' himself, and who was pleased to acknowledge most graciously those expressions of their loyalty and devotion, by bowing, grinning, and clapping his paws. Having administered to the *bride* some preliminary instructions, the impatient wives desired him to remain by the pool's side until they should commune with his Satanic Highness on the subject of *her* inauguration, directing *her*, as they proceeded on their voyage across the pool, to speed them in their master's name. To this order of the black pair the *bride* was resolved to pay particular attention. As soon as they were embarked in their riddles, and had wriggled themselves, by means of their brooms, into a proper depth of water, 'Go,' says he, 'in the name of the Best.' A horrid yell from the witches announced their instant fate,—the magic spell was now dissolved—crash went the riddles, and down sank the two witches, never more to rise, amidst the shrieks and lamentations of the Old Thief and all his infernal crew, whose combined power and policy could not save them from a watery end. All the torches were extinguished in an instant, and the affrighted company fled in different directions, in such forms and similitudes as they thought most convenient for them to adopt; and the *wily bride* returned home at his leisure, enjoying himself vastly at the clever manner in which he had executed the instructions of his deceased friends. On arriving at his house, he dressed himself in his own clothes, and, without immediately satisfying his wife's curiosity at the result of his excursion, he yoked his cattle, and commenced his morning labours with as little concern as usual. His two neighbours, who were not even conscious of the absence of their wives, (so ably substituted were they by the brooms,) did the same. Towards breakfast-time, however, the two neighbours were not a little astonished that they observed no signs of their wives having risen from bed—notwithstanding their customary earliness— and this surprise they, expressed to the *late bride*, their neighbour. The latter archly remarked, that he had great suspicions, in his own mind, of their *rising* even that day. 'What mean you by that?' replied they. 'We left our wives apparently in good health when we ourselves arose.'—'Find them now,' was the reply—the bride setting up as merry a whistle as before. Running each to his bed, what was the astonishment of the husbands, when, instead of his wife, he only found an old broom. Their neighbour then told them, that, if they chose to examine Pol-nain well, they would find both their dear doxies there. The grieving husbands accordingly proceeded thither, and, with the necessary instruments, dragged their late worthy partners to dry land; and afterwards privately interred them. The shattered vessels and oars of those unfortunate navigators, whirling about the pool, satisfied their lords of the manner by which they came to their *ends*; and their names were no longer mentioned by their kindred in the land. It need scarcely be added, that the poor man gradually recovered his former opulence; and that, in the course of a short time, he was comparatively as rich as he was formerly poor."

CHAPTER III.
OF THE PERSONAL SIMILITUDE OF THE AGENTS OR MEMBERS OF THE CRAFT.

IT is well known, that no sooner do men or women enter on this profession, than there is a striking change in their personal appearance. Their countenances are no longer the emblems of human nature, but the sign-posts of malice and bad luck. "Looking like a witch" is a proverb that has been always descriptive of the most exquisite ugliness; and whoever has seen the frontispiece of a Highland witch will be satisfied with its force and propriety.

The face is so wrinkled, that it commonly resembles the channels of dried waters, and the colour of it resembles nothing so much as a piece of rough tanned leather. The eyes are small and piercing, sunk into the forehead, like the expiring remains of a candle in a socket. The nose is large, prominent, and sharp, forming a bridge to the contacting chin. These are represented as the amiable features of a witch. The wizard's appearance differs very little from that of his amiable sister the witch, only that his face is covered over with a preternatural redundance of hair, and that he wears beneath his chin a bunch of hair in the manner of a goat.

It has been long a subject of tough controversy to what cause this striking deformity is justly to be ascribed. Some logicians rationally enough maintain, that the characteristic deformity of the order arises from their frequent interviews with Satan; that the tremor of the limbs, the horror of the aspect, and stare of the eyes, with which they are always seized during the season of their noviciation, are rendered habitual to them by the force of custom, which is justly called a second nature. And, in support of this doctrine, we are told it is a fact, that, whenever we behold a ghost, or any other *uncanny* being, our features become contracted exactly the same way. But, be this as it may, it is an acknowledged fact, that ugliness was, from the beginning of their cast, their distinguishing characteristic.

CHAPTER IV.
OF THEIR PROFESSIONAL POWERS AND PRACTICES.

ON a nearer examination of a witch's character, we will find her face a very correct index to her heart. She is the arch-enemy of whatever is good and amiable. Invested as she is with as ample powers of seduction and mischief as Satan himself, she is equally expert in accomplishing the ruin of the soul and body of the objects of her malignity. In order to convey to the reader an idea of those powers with which she is invested, and which she never fails to exercise, we shall detail them in their order, illustrating our statements, as we go along, with proofs from the best authorities.

The most formidable of all the powers conferred on a witch consists in the torture and destruction of human beings by infernal machination. There are various processes by which those hellish practices are accomplished, but the most common process is that invented and used by that eminent and distinguished witch, *"Crea Mhoir cun Drochdair,"* who was burnt and worried at a stake at Inverness, about two centuries ago, for bewitching and keeping in torment the body of the provost's son. Crea made an effigy of clay and other hellish ingredients, into which she stuck pins and other sharp instruments. This effigy of the provost's son she placed on a spit at a large fire, and by these cantrips the hag communicated such agonizing torments to the young gentleman, that he must have had speedily fallen a victim to his sufferings, had it not been for the happy discovery made by means of a little grandchild of Crea Mhoir's, who divulged the whole secret to a little companion, for the small gratification of a piece of bread and cheese. But although Crea, honest woman, was long ago disposed of, to the great comfort and satisfaction of her countrymen, who naturally enough ascribed to her all the calamities which happened in the country during her lifetime, she left behind her the immortal fruits of her genius, for the benefit of her black posterity, in those mischievous inventions practised by the witches of latter times, who understand the knack of torturing their unhappy contemporaries in all its branches, as exemplified in the cases of several worthies noticed in the sequel.

The next important power of a witch and a warlock consists in their control over air and water, whereby they raise most dreadful storms and hurricanes by sea and by land, and thus accomplish the destruction of many a valuable life, which otherwise might have been long spared. The following account of the loss of a most excellent gentleman exhibits too melancholy an instance of the success of their experiments in this way:

"John Garve Macgillichallum of Razay was an ancient hero of great celebrity. Distinguished in the age in which he lived for the gallantry of his exploits, he has often been selected by the bard as the theme of his poems and songs. Alongst with a constitution of body naturally vigorous and powerful, Razay was gifted with all those noble qualities of the mind which a true hero is supposed to possess. And what reflected additional lustre on his character, was that he never failed to apply his talents and powers to the best uses. He was the active and inexorable enemy of the weird sisterhood, many of whom he was the auspicious instrument of sending to their 'black inheritance' much sooner than they either expected or desired. It was not therefore to be supposed, that, while those amiable actions endeared Razay to all good people, they were at all calculated to win him the regard of those infernal hags to whom he was so deadly a foe. As might be naturally expected, they cherished towards him the most implacable thirst of revenge, and sought, with unremitting vigilance, for an opportunity of quenching it. That such an opportunity did unhappily occur, and that the meditated revenge of these hags was too well accomplished, will speedily appear from this melancholy story.

"It happened upon a time that Razay and a number of friends planned an expedition to the island of Lewes, for the purpose of hunting the deer of that place. They accordingly embarked on board the chieftain's yacht, manned by the flower of the young men of Razay, and in a few hours they chased the fleet-bounding hart on the mountains of Lewes. Their sport proved excellent. Hart after hart, and hind after hind, were soon levelled to the ground by the unerring hand of Razay; and when night terminated the chase, they retired to their shooting quarters, where they spent the night with joviality, and mirth, little dreaming of their melancholy fate in the morning.

"In the morning of next day, the chief of Razay and his followers rose with the sun, with the view of returning to Razay. The day was squally and occasionally boisterous, and the billows raged with great violence. But Razay was determined to cross the channel to his residence, and ordered his yacht to prepare for the voyage. The more cautious and less courageous of his suite, however, urged on him to defer the expedition till the weather should somewhat settle—an advice which Razay, with a courage which knew no fear, rejected, and expressed his firm determination to proceed without delay. Probably with a view to inspire his company with the necessary degree of courage to induce them all to concur in the undertaking, he adjourned with them to the ferry-house, where they had recourse to that supporter of spirits under every trial, the usquebaugh, a few bottles of which added vastly to the resolution of the company. Just as the party were disputing the practicability of the proposed adventure, an old woman, with wrinkled front, bending on a crutch, entered the ferry-house; and Razay, in the heat of argument, appealed to the old woman, whether the passage of the channel on such a day was not perfectly practicable and free from danger. The woman, without hesitation, replied in the affirmative, adding such observations, reflecting on their courage, as immediately silenced every opposition to the voyage; and accordingly the whole party embarked in the yacht for Razay. But, alas! what were the consequences? No sooner were they abandoned to the mercy of the waves than the elements seemed to conspire to their destruction. All attempts to put back the vessel proved unavailing, and she was speedily driven out before the wind in the direction of Razay. The heroic chieftain laboured hard to animate his company, and to dispel the despair which began to seize them, by the most exemplary courage and resolution. He took charge of the helm, and, in spite of the combined efforts of the sea, wind, and lightning, he kept the vessel steadily on her course towards the lofty point of Aird in Skye. The drooping spirits of his crew began to revive, and hope began to smile upon them—when lo! to their great astonishment, a large cat was seen to climb the rigging. This cat was soon followed by another of equal size, and the last by a successor, until at length the shrouds, masts, and whole tackle, were actually covered with them. Nor did the sight of all those cats, although he knew well enough their real character, intimidate the resolute Razay, until a large black cat, larger than any of the rest, appeared on the masthead, as commander-in-chief of the whole legion. Razay, on observing him, instantly foresaw the result; he, however, determined to sell his life as dearly as possible, and immediately commanded an attack upon the cats—but, alas! it soon proved abortive. With a simultaneous effort the cats overturned the vessel on her leeward wale, and every soul on board was precipitated into a watery grave. Thus ended the glorious life of *Jan Garbh Macgillichallum* of Razay, to the lasting regret of the brave clan Leod and all good people, and to the great satisfaction of the abominable witches who thus accomplished his lamentable doom.

"The same day, another hero, celebrated for his hatred of witchcraft, was warming himself in his hunting hut, in the forest of Gaick in Badenoch. His faithful hounds, fatigued with the morning chase, lay stretched on the turf by his side,—his gun, that would not miss, reclined in the neuk of the boothy,—the *skian dhu* of the sharp edge hung by his side, and these alone constituted his company. As the hunter sat listening to the howling storm as it whistled by, there entered at the door an apparently poor weather-beaten cat, shivering with cold, and drenched to the skin. On observing her, the hairs of the dogs became erected bristles, and they immediately rose to attack the pitiable cat, which stood trembling at the door. 'Great hunter of the hills,' exclaims the poor-looking trembling cat, 'I claim your protection. I know your hatred to my craft, and perhaps it is just. Still spare, oh spare a poor jaded wretch, who thus flies to you for protection from the cruelty and oppression of her sisterhood.' Moved to compassion by her eloquent address, and disdaining to take advantage of his greatest enemy in such a seemingly forlorn situation, he pacified his infuriated dogs, and desired her to come forward to the fire and warm herself. 'Nay,' says she, 'in the first place, you will please bind with this long hair those two furious hounds of yours, for I am afraid they will tear my poor hams to pieces. I pray you, therefore, my dear sir, that you would have the goodness to bind them together by the necks with this long hair.' But the curious nature of the hair induced the hunter to dissemble a little. Instead of having bound his dogs with it, as he pretended, he threw it across a beam of wood which connected the couple of the boothy. The witch then supposing the dogs securely bound, approached the fire, and squatted herself down as if to dry herself. She had not sitten many minutes, when the hunter could easily discover a striking increase in her size, which he could not forbear remarking in a jocular manner to herself. 'A bad death to you, you nasty beast,' says the hunter; 'you are getting very large.'—'Aye, aye,' replied the cat, equally jocosely, 'as my hairs imbibe the heat, they naturally expand.' These jokes, however, were but a prelude to a more serious conversation. The cat still continuing her growth, had at length attained a most extraordinary size,—when, in the twinkling of an eye, she transformed herself into her proper likeness of the Goodwife of Laggan, and thus addressed him: 'Hunter of the Hills, your hour of reckoning is arrived. Behold me before you, the avowed champion of my devoted sisterhood, of whom Macgillichallum of Razay and you were always the most relentless enemies. But Razay is no more. His last breath is fled. He lies a lifeless corpse on the bottom of the main; and now, Hunter of the Hills, it is your turn.' With these words, assuming a most hideous and terrific appearance, she made a spring at the hunter. The two dogs, which she supposed securely bound by the infernal hair, sprung at her in her turn, and a most furious conflict ensued. The witch, thus unexpectedly attacked by the dogs, now began to repent of her temerity. '*Fasten, hair, fasten,*' she perpetually exclaimed, supposing the dogs to have been bound by the hair; and so effectually did the hair *fasten*, according to her order, that it at last snapt the beam in twain. At length, finding herself completely overpowered, she attempted a retreat, but so closely were the hounds fastened in her breasts, that it was with no small difficulty she could get herself disengaged from them. Screaming and shrieking, the Wife of Laggan dragged herself out of the house, trailing after the dogs, which were fastened in her so closely, that they never loosed their hold until she demolished every tooth in their heads. Then metamorphosing herself into the likeness of a raven, she fled over the mountains in the direction of her home. The two faithful dogs, bleeding and exhausted, returned to their master, and, in the act of caressing his hand, both fell down and expired at his feet. Regretting their loss with a sorrow only known to the parent who weeps over the remains of departed children, he buried his devoted dogs, and returned home to his family. His wife was not in the house when he arrived, but she soon made her appearance. 'Where have you been, my love?' inquired the husband.— 'Indeed,' replies she, 'I have been seeing the Goodwife of Laggan, who has been just seized with so severe an illness, that she is not expected to live for any time.'—'Aye! aye!' says he, 'what is the matter with the worthy woman?'—'She was all day absent in the moss at her peats,' replies the wife, 'and was seized with a sudden colic, in consequence of getting wet feet, and now all her friends and neighbours are expecting her demision.'— 'Poor woman,' says the husband, 'I am sorry for her. Get me some dinner, it will be right that I should go and see her also.' Dinner being provided and dispatched, the hunter immediately proceeded to the house of Laggan, where he found a great assemblage of neighbours mourning, with great sincerity, the approaching decease of a woman whom they all had hitherto esteemed virtuous. The hunter, walking up to the sick woman's bed in a rage, proportioned to the greatness of its cause, stripped the sick woman of all her coverings. A shriek from the now exposed witch brought all the company around her. 'Behold,' says he, 'the object of your solicitude, who is nothing less than an infernal witch. To-day, she informs me, she was present at the death of the Laird of Razay, and only a few hours have elapsed since she attempted to make me share his fate. This night, however, she shall expiate her crime, by the forfeiture of her horrid life.' Relating to the company the whole circumstances of her attack upon him, which were too well corroborated by the conclusive marks she bore on her person, the whole company were perfectly convinced of her criminality; and the customary punishment was about to be inflicted on her, when the miserable wretch addressed them as follows: 'My ill-requited friends, spare an old acquaintance, already in the agonies of death, from any farther mortal degradation. My crimes and my folly now stare me in the face, in their true colours, while my vile and perfidious seducer, the enemy of your temporal and spiritual interests, only laughs at me in my distress; and, as a reward for my fidelity to his interest, in seducing every thing that was amiable, and in destroying every thing that was good, he is now about to consign my soul to eternal misery. Let my example be a warning to all the people of the earth to shun the fatal rock on which I have split; and as a strong inducement for them to do so, I shall atone for my iniquity to the utmost of my ability, by detailing to you the awful history of my life.' Here the Wife of Laggan detailed at full length the way she was seduced into the service of the evil one,—all the criminal adventures in which she had been engaged, and ended with a particular account of the death of Macgillichallum of Razay, and her attack upon the hunter, and then expired.

"Meanwhile, a neighbour of the Wife of Laggan was returning home late at night from Strathdearn, where he had been upon some business, and had just entered the dreary forest of Monalea in Badenoch, when he met a woman dressed in black, who ran with great speed, and inquired of the traveller, with great agitation, how far she was distant from the church-yard of Dalarossie, and if she could be there by twelve o'clock. The traveller told her she might, if she continued to go at the same pace that she did then. She then fled alongst the road, uttering the most desponding lamentations, and the traveller continued his road to Badenoch. He had not, however, walked many miles when he met a large black dog, which travelled past him with much velocity, as if upon the scent of a track or footsteps, and soon after he met another large black dog sweeping along in the same manner. The last dog, however, was scarcely past, when he met a stout black man on a fine fleet black courser, prancing along in the same direction after the dogs. 'Pray,' says the rider to the traveller, 'did you meet a woman as you came along the hill?' The traveller replied in the affirmative. 'And did you meet a dog soon after?' rejoined the rider. The traveller replied he did. 'And,' added the rider, 'do you think the dog will overtake her ere she can reach the church of Dalarossie?'—'He will, at any rate, be very close upon her heels,' answered the traveller. Each then took his own way. But before the traveller had got the length of Glenbanchar, the rider overtook him on his return, with the foresaid woman before him across the bow of his saddle, and one of the dogs fixed in her breast, and another in her thigh. 'Where did you overtake the woman?' inquired the traveller. 'Just as she was entering the church-yard of Dalarossie,' was his reply. On the traveller's return home, he heard of the fate of the unfortunate Wife of Laggan, which soon explained the nature of the company he had met on the road. It was, no doubt, the spirit of the Wife of Laggan flying for protection from the infernal spirits, (to whom she had sold herself,) to the church-yard of Dalarossie, which is so sacred a place, that a witch is immediately dissolved from all her ties with Satan, on making a pilgrimage to it, either dead or alive. But it seems the unhappy Wife of Laggan was a stage too late."

There is another power given to them, which is a most mischievous one, and proves the fruitful source of almost all the crimes and miseries which deluge the land,—that of sowing the seeds of discord amongst mankind in public and private life. We will say nothing of the degree of secret influence which these worthies probably enjoy in overruling the councils of our nation, and thwarting the judgment of our ministers, so as to answer their private purposes, as it would be out of our strict line of delineation. But we speak from the best authority when we say, that they are the common and secret instigators of those deplorable quarrels and divisions which sometimes happen between those who ought to be one flesh. Whenever we see a broken-hearted wife mourning over the misconduct of her husband, who, once tenderly affectionate and attentive to the discharge of his domestic duties, is now changed into the domestic tyrant and whisky-bibber, we need never hesitate for a moment to pronounce the cause to be witchcraft. And the same rule holds good in regard to the misconduct of the wife, *vice versa*. Behold, again, the man of sin, clothed in the garment of disgrace, that sits *"girnan on the creepy."* Ask him what blind-fold infatuation could have induced him to have defiled his neighbour's bed, and he will tell you, with a groan, it was *"Buchuchd."*

Nor are their operations confined to the injury of a person's spiritual interest alone—they even descend to the lowest incidents in a man's calling. If the reader should see a termagant of a wife raise over the *caput* of her poor cuckold of a husband the tongs or spurtle, demanding of him, with vehement eloquence, the cause of purchasing a horse or a cow at double its value, his answer to her will certainly be—"Me ve ar mu Buchuchd."

Thus the ruination of our spiritual interest is not enough to satisfy their inveterate malignity,—they must likewise injure our temporal interests, which, however incomparable to the former in point of intrinsic importance, yet cause the sufferer fully as much grief. Indeed, so dearly do the most of the people of this world love their temporal means and estate, that we feel fully persuaded, that did those agents confine their operations to the injury of our spiritual interests alone, which, as Satan's instruments, we should naturally suppose to be their proper line of business, the clamour against their ruinous and abominable practices would be much less violent than it is. This much, however, of the Highlander's liberal disposition the sly sounding witch is intimately acquainted with, and for this very reason she redoubles her diligence to cause him all the loss in her power, as the most effectual way of completing his misery. Hence it oftens happens, that should a horse, an ox, or a cow, of unequalled symmetry and beauty, be so unlucky as to attract the favour of its affectionate owner;—by whatever means the sagacious witch discovers the secret we know not, but certain annihilation, accomplished by some means or other, will be the poor animal's lot. Such a calamity as this is sufficiently mortifying, but it is a small one when compared to the loss of a person's whole stock, which too frequently follows the loss of one. Having once inserted the infernal pillow into some snug corner, its influence will give the finishing stroke to all the cattle and creeping things on a farm. This pillow, not to give it a worse name, is a little four-cornered *bag*, packed with divers exterminating diseases, in the familiar likeness of hair, grease, parings of nails, shoe tackets, salt, powder, and other infernal knick-knacks, too tedious to be described, which, when thrown into the fire, makes a noise the like of which has seldom been heard.

No sooner is this bag deposited in a cleft in the stable or byre than it commences its destructive career, producing the death of the bestial in whole lots, until the last hen on the roost will fall a sacrifice to its deadly influence. Nor is this all; they will attach some infernal cantrips to the farming-utensils that no good crop will follow their operations, and what may escape the influence of the *baggie* is commonly destroyed by frost, rain, lightning, and other calamities, which the craft can produce at their pleasure, so that it is unfit for the use of man or beast. In short, of all the ills incident to the life of man, none are so formidable as witchcraft, before the combined influence of which, to use the language of an honest man who had himself severely suffered from its effects, "the great Laird of Grant himself could not stand them if they should fairly yoke upon him."

CHAPTER V.
OF THE WITCH'S POWERS OF TRANSFORMATION.

THOSE of our readers who are not very well acquainted with the theory of witchcraft will not be a little surprised, at the unaccountable activity of its agents, who are capable of paying not only proper attention to their own private affairs, but likewise of carrying on almost all the business of the Evil One in this land. In order to obviate all surprise on this head, be it remembered, that they are endowed with as ample powers of transmigration (at their institution into the craft) as any other of Satan's spiritual agents; consequently there is no similitude from their own proper likenesses to that of a cat or a stone, but they can assume at pleasure. Hence the speed and privacy with which they attain their evil ends.

One of the most ordinary disguises of a "*Ban-Buchichd*" is the similitude of a hare. This transformation she finds exceedingly convenient while performing her cantrips in the field—bewitching farming implements— destroying corn and grass—holding communion with the sisterhood, and similar pieces of business. It enables her to execute her undertakings with greater expedition, and flee more fleetly on any emergency, than she could do in any other character.

A second is the likeness of a cat—by personating which, she procures admission to the inmost recesses of a house, to deposit her infernal machinery, without exciting the least suspicions of her real character and intentions.

A third is her transformation into a stone, which is a common practice with the witch in the season of agricultural operations, by which she is afforded great opportunities of mischief to the farmer's interest. The wily witch will penetrate into the ground, and place herself in the line of the plough, and as it passes her she will creep in betwixt the sock and the culter. The plough is consequently expelled from the ground for a considerable space, and a "*bauk*" is the consequence. For these insidious and barefaced acts of iniquity, the witch, if discovered, seldom escapes with impunity. Stopping the cattle, the ploughman will take hold of the stone, bestowing upon it the most abusive and opprobrious epithets, and dashes her with all his might against the hardest substance he can find, as a mark of his hatred and contempt for her character.

A fourth is her transformation into the shape of a raven; which now in a great measure supersedes the use of her ancient and renowned hobby-horse the broom, on which she formerly walloped with such surprising velocity. This similitude is commonly assumed by her when on excursions to any distance, to attend the counsels of Satan—to hold communion with the sisterhood—or to attend some important enterprise.

The witch likewise assumes the character of a *magpie* on occasions of sudden emergency which require immediate conference with a number of the members of the craft. The likeness of this bird, which is of a domestic character, and fond of hopping and picking about the doors, screens the witch from suspicion, as she visits another witch's dwelling. Hence, when a number of magpies convene together side by side on a house-top, it is no wonder that their appearance should occasionally excite suspicion. But we humbly think that mere suspicion by no means justifies that hostility of temper which in several districts the inhabitants are led to entertain against the whole race of magpies, merely because the witches sometimes assume their similitude. These suspicions are no doubt a good deal heightened by the circumstance of the poor magpie's being a little endowed with the gift of prophecy. As a foreteller of minor events—such as the coming of visitors, the change of weather, and such-like little occurrences—the magpie has never been excelled; and notwithstanding the illiberal conduct of its human neighbours, those little qualities are always exerted by the magpie for their comfort and convenience.

On the morning of that auspicious day on which the factor, the parson, or any other of the country gentry of equal importance, is to pay a visit to the lord of the manor on which the magpie may have pitched her residence, she will approach the house, and, by her incessant chattering, announce to the inhabitants the coming of the consequential stranger. The state apartment, perhaps rather deranged, is consequently arrayed in proper order; and the necessary provisions to entertain the expected guests are timeously procured, which, but for the magpie's generous and ill-rewarded premonition, could not perhaps be provided for the occasion.

CHAPTER VI.
SAFEGUARDS FROM WITCHCRAFT.

AS witchcraft is in itself by far the greatest calamity the Highlander is subject to, so Providence, in its wise economy, has afforded him the amplest means of guarding against its effects. And if a radical remedy has not yet been discovered for the evil in all its bearings, it is only because mankind have not been equally solicitous for the discovery of it. Adverse to a murmuring discontented spirit, the Highlander is satisfied with the removal of a share of his grievances. Having obtained a knowledge of a certain remedy for those practices of the craft which weigh most heavily on his temporal interests, he is not so presumptuous as to suppose that Providence is so partial in its favours as to grant him a remedy for those that affect his immortal interests also. Satisfied with the benefits he enjoys, he is not clamorous for an extension of them, leaving the concerns of another world for a season of more convenience and leisure.

As a sovereign protection for goods and chattels of every description from the machinations of those despicable agents, the rowan cross, of invaluable excellence, has never been known to prove ineffectual. Its salutary influence on every species of supernatural agents is well known, and there are none to whom the smell of the rowan is more obnoxious than the "Ban Buchuchd." As a proof of its efficacy, we can produce no better authority than the following affecting story:—

"There is, in the vicinity of Forres, an old decayed edifice, called '*Castle Boorgie*,' in which once lived a rich laird, who had a beautiful daughter. Seemingly possessed of every engaging accomplishment, and apparently endowed with the most amiable disposition, she was the darling of her aged father, whose hopes and joys were wholly centered in her. One spring morning, as her father and herself were surveying the delightful prospects which the castle commanded, the immense number of ploughs at work within the compass of their vision happened to attract their attention. 'Father,' says this ill-fated, unconscious child, 'do we not behold a vast number of ploughs in the widely-extended district now in our view?'—'Yes, my love, we do,' replied the father, 'and it is a pleasant thing to look at them.'—'What reward will you give me,' added she, 'if, by a single word, I shall cause them all stand as immoveable as if the cattle were transformed into stones?'—'On that condition,' replied the astonished father, 'the most superb and costly gown in the town of Forres shall be yours.'—'It is done,' says the daughter. Raising her hand, she muttered an unintelligible sound, and, lo! all the ploughs in the district, with the exception of a single one, stood stock still and immoveable.—'Indeed!' exclaims the father, 'you are a rare conjuror, my dear; but how is that plough in the adjacent park exempted from the magical effect of your powerful charm?'—'The cause I can easily guess,' says she; 'there is, in one of the oxen's bows, a pin of the rowan tree, the virtue of which defeats all attempts at preternatural fascination.'—'Aye, aye,' says he, 'all those things are wonderfully pretty; pray who taught them to you?'—'My old nurse taught me those fine things, and am not I greatly obliged to her, sir?'—'You are, undoubtedly,' he replies, 'and she shall soon have her reward. Oh! my dear, my only child— support and comfort of my aged head—would to God you had never been born!'

"Summoning immediately a council of his friends, the broken-hearted parent revealed to them the whole circumstance, and craved their opinion as to the measures that should be adopted in this deeply-to-be-deplored case. After due consultation, the council gave it as their decided opinion, that, concluding that she was irrecoverably lost to all good in this world, the extension of her life would be only productive of eternal disgrace and infamy to her friends, while her spiritual interests would every day be destroyed by accumulating guilt. Therefore, that her life should be instantly terminated by a private death; and that the old hag, the author of her ruin, should be publicly burned under every ignominious circumstance. To this hard decision the agonised father was persuaded to assent; and a doctor was immediately dispatched for to Forres, to point out the easiest mode of taking her life. Bleeding the temporal arteries was the mode of death agreed on, and the poor innocent victim of the old hag's depravity was introduced into a private apartment, in order to undergo the awful operation. On entering the apartment, her unhappy father burst out into a flood of tears. Observing his distress, his affectionate little daughter also fell a crying. 'What is the matter with you, my dear father?' says she. 'Have you received any bad news? Oh! tell me what is the matter with you, that I may share your sorrows and dry your tears.' Fearing that the father's courage might naturally fail him under so signal a trial, the friends present instantly seized the astonished dear girl, bound her hand and foot, and placed her in a vat, and the surgeon inflicted on her two brows, fair and beautiful as those of an angel, the fatal wounds. As the blood flowed, the poor affrighted victim perpetually exclaimed, 'Do not kill me, do not kill me; what have I done to offend my dearest father? I am sure I did no harm. For the sake of my dear mother, who is no more, and for whose sake you loved me so well, do not let them kill me, my dear father.' The unhappy father sunk senseless on the floor, and his expiring child soon closed her eyes on this world, sighing, with her last breath, 'My dearest father, do not kill me.'

"The old hag was then brought out to the lawn in front of the castle, and thrown into a huge furnace of tar and other combustibles, amidst the general execration of the assembled multitude. And it is said, that while the witch was burning, every crack she gave was as loud as the report of a war cannon."

When, by the neglect of the prescribed safeguards, the seeds of iniquity have taken root, and a person's means are decaying in consequence, the only alternative, in this case, is to resort to that grand remedy, the "*Tein Econuch*," or "*Forlorn Fire*," which seldom fails of being productive of the best effects. The cure for witchcraft, called "*Tein Econuch*," is wrought in the following manner:—

A consultation being held by the unhappy sufferer and his friends as to the most advisable measures of effecting a cure, if this process is adopted, notice is privately communicated to all those householders who reside within the nearest two running streams, to extinguish their lights and fires on some appointed morning. On its being ascertained that this notice has been duly observed, a spinning-wheel, or some other convenient instrument, calculated to produce fire by friction, is set to work with the most furious earnestness by the unfortunate sufferer and all who wish well to his cause. Relieving each other by turns, they drive on with such persevering diligence, that at length the spindle of the wheel, ignited by excessive friction, emits "*Forlorn Fire*" in abundance, which, by the application of tow, or some other combustible material, is widely extended over the whole neighbourhood. Communicating the fire to the tow, the tow communicates it to a candle, the candle to a fir-torch, the torch to a cartful of peats, which the master of the ceremonies, with pious ejaculations for the success of the experiment, distributes to messengers, who will proceed with portions of it to the different houses within the said two running streams, to kindle the different fires. By the influence of this operation, the machinations and spells of witchcraft "are rendered null and void," and, in the language of Scots' law, "of no avail, force, strength, or effect, with all that has followed, or may follow thereupon."

But should the evil prove so obstinate and deep-rooted as to triumph over this most commonly efficacious remedy, the dernier resort is an application to that arch-enemy of Satan, Mr. Grigor Willox Macgrigor, Emperor of all the Conjurors.

The name of this gentleman is well known to the inhabitants of the northern counties of Scotland, as the happy proprietor of that invaluable and wonderful relic, which the vulgar are sometimes pleased to denominate "Clach Ghrigair Willock," alias "*Clach Ban na Buchuchd*," but which, in our opinion, deserves a far more dignified, if not a more appropriate appellation. We humbly submit it should be called the *Philosopher's Stone*, not so much out of compliment to its learned and elegant proprietor— although, by the bye, he is wonderfully *philosophic*—as out of pure justice to the stone itself; for it certainly is the best substitute for the grand object of the chemist's research that has hitherto been discovered. If the philosopher's stone will convert metal into gold, the "warlock's stone" will convert water into silver by a process perhaps more round-about, but equally certain.

The history of such a precious curiosity as this would, no doubt, prove highly interesting to the "curious reader;" and the writer has to blame the shortness of his memory for not gratifying him to the utmost of his wish, Mr. Willox having more than once personally favoured him with a very eloquent account of it. Suffice it to say, that this stone was originally extorted by a very ancient ancestor of Mr. Willox from an amorous slut of a mermaid, who, unfortunately for her, happened to take a fancy to him, and no wonder, too, if he possessed in any degree the personal attractions of his lineal posterity. It happened, then, that this silly fool of a mermaid once thought it proper to throw herself in this gentleman's way, expecting, no doubt, very different treatment from that which she experienced,—when her unnatural sweetheart, instead of offering her any endearments, most ungraciously chained her to a post, until she redeemed her liberty by this precious ransom. This was, no doubt, long, long ago, nobody knows how long, and the *stone* has necessarily seen many revolutions of times and masters in the course of its day. It graced for a long time the warlike standard of the brave clan Gregor, combining, as the upholsterer says, "great ornament with much utility;" for, while it served to set off not a little those splendid banners, it invariably secured their followers victory over their contending foes. It afterwards returned to the Willox family, with whom it has continued to the present day. It could not descend to a race of gentlemen who could do greater justice to its excellent qualities, and certainly the fault cannot be traced to the present proprietor, if, during his liferent use of it, the stone has lost an iota of its former celebrity.

Whatever might have been the ornamental qualities of this wonderful *stone* in the days of yore, it has now no great ornaments to boast of. It is a plain-looking article, strongly resembling the knob or bottom of a crystal bottle; and were it not that Mr. Willox solemnly assured us of his having been told by the great Lord Henderland himself, it must have at one time composed one of the Pleiades, we should have had much difficulty in believing it to consist of any other substance; but who could resist such respectable authority? Although Mr. Willox informed us that a single collision with the ground would instantly divest it of all its wonderful virtues, the stone certainly bears *ex facie* marks of rough usage, and even such inauspicious accidents as coming into contact with the ground, or perhaps harder materials, in its time. However, the *stone* itself will tell no secrets, and on the subject of accidents of this sort it is the proprietor's interest to be equally mute.

But whatever may be the nature and qualities of this stone, its virtues are sufficiently notorious. A single immersion of it into a hogshead of water instantaneously communicates to it such inconceivable virtue, that one drop of it is sufficient to cure the most desperate case of witchcraft in the land. Nor do the prevention and cure of witchcraft alone constitute the stone's sole line of business;—for a valuable reward, there is no secret or calamity natural to man or beast in all this wide world, but it will reveal or prevent.—*Exemple gratia*: should some miserable vagabond of a thief, residing within the pale of Mr. Willox's celebrity, be so fool-hardy as to lay his dishonest hands upon the goods or chattels of a neighbour, recovery of the goods, or at least an exposure of the thief, is the absolute consequence. The loser of the goods looks about him for his purse, and immediately proceeds to consult the GRAND ORACLE, Mr. Grigor Willox, as to the person who had the effrontery to steal his goods. Mr. Willox, willing to afford every information on reasonable terms, instantly produces the black stocking containing the stone, a single dip of which clearly developes the whole circumstance. After a long consultation, involving some inquiries as to suspected characters, the lynx-eyed Mr. Willox easily recognises some figures reflected on the vessel containing the water by the stone, conveying an exact representation of some old hag not very reputable for her habits, residing in the complainant's neighbourhood; and thus all doubt is removed as to his suspicions being too well founded.

It is no subject for wonder, then, that this Great Oracle should be so highly prized and suitably encouraged. With commendable regard to the good of his beloved countrymen, Mr. Willox is in the habit of *occasionally* making a tour of pleasure through the counties of Inverness, Ross, and Caithness, whence, after some weeks' absence, he returns home, with the double satisfaction of thinking, that while he has, in the course of his rambles, conferred the greatest benefit on suffering humanity, he has, at the same time, a good deal improved his own pecuniary resources. Those occasional peregrinations of this gentleman are now become absolutely necessary. Funds are not only very low in these bad times, but Mr. Willox is convinced more and more, every day he rises, of the truth of that proverb, "A prophet has no honour in his own country;" and he therefore finds it no less his interest than his duty to take a trip, as occasion suggests, to see his friends in the *Duigh Tua*. For the most part, however, he resides at his seat of Gaulrig in Strathavon (usually called Strathdown), where, like the late Doctor Samuel Solomon, inventor and proprietor of that renovating cordial the Balm of Gilead, he may be consulted, either personally or by letter post paid, on payment of the usual compliment of a pound note. Accordingly, there are pilgrimages made to Gaulrig as well as to Gilead House. It is no rare matter for the inhabitants of both sides of the Avon to fall in with unfortunate pilgrims, whose longitude of face and decrepitude of limbs indicate the extent of their misfortunes and the length of their journey, inquiring the way for *Taigh Maishter Willack.*

PART VII.
Highland Festive Amusements.

Yes, let the rich deride, the proud disdain,

The simple pleasures of the lowly train;

To me more dear, congenial to my heart,

One native charm, than all the gloss of art.

GOLDSMITH.

HALLOWE'EN.

Ye powers of darkness and of hell,

Propitious to the magic spell,

Who rule in silence o'er the night,

Be present now.

FRANCES.

OF the whole series of annual festivals, Hallowe'en forms the most important occasion in the Highlands of Scotland. The fascinating round of varied enjoyments the night presents to the young and juvenile—the delightful peeps into futurity it affords to the enchanted lover—and the fond recollections it revives in old age—all conspire to render its approach more interesting, and its celebration more joyful, than any other occasion within the compass of the year. Nor is the happy influence diffused by Hallowe'en confined to the human class of the inhabitants of the Highlands alone; most of the *supernatural inhabitants* are in some degree partakers in the general happiness. With the fairy community, in particular, it is an occasion of peculiar grandeur, as the great anniversary on which they are reviewed by *Auld Nick*, their nominal chief potentate, in person; whilst many others of the classes treated of in the foregoing pages regard it as a night of no ordinary pomp and joviality.

On this occasion of universal hilarity, the natural coldness and jealousy which generally subsist between the human species and their supernatural neighbours are changed into perfect harmony and benevolence. Like two belligerent armies, whose hostility towards each other is more the offspring of public duty than private resentment, and who, therefore, during the intervals of war, exhibit in their mutual intercourse the marks of personal good will; so, in like manner, those two classes forget for the night all animosity, in their more laudable zeal to contribute to each other's gratification. Nay, stern Satan himself relaxes for this night his avarice; and, alive to no other object than the promotion of universal enjoyments, dispatches showers of his emissaries to the several kiln-pots, peat-stacks, and barn-yards in the Highlands, to afford to those adventurers who desire it a peep into the secrets of futurity.

Such a display of seeming benevolence, did it proceed from any other individual than Satan, could not fail to meet with some share of applause. But heads of families, whose opinions are entitled to some respect, have been known to affirm, that Satan's affected generosity on this occasion is nothing but a mere stratagem for inveigling the more effectually the young and unwary into his vile snares, and that he gets more game by those specious artifices than he could realize by any other means. Hence it is that the anxious parent this night, instead of extolling Satan's generosity, is so intent on magnifying his perfidy; and in order the better to dissuade his offspring and family from the dangerous practices of the night, details, without qualification, his numerous treacheries on similar occasions.

But these ebullitions of the parent's jealousy of Satan's practices are soon subdued. The big-bellied bottle and bumper-glass will have a great effect in relaxing his heart of its illiberal suspicions. Speedily animated by the conciliating qualities of the "*barley-bree*," and softened by the recollection of his own youthful frolics and manly deeds on similar occasions, he no longer regards as a crime those practices which he recently condemned; and the good-natured matron, being happy at her husband's felicity, and averse to chide, they both tacitly connive at the family's indulgence in the customary arts of divination.

Generally the first spell they try is pulling the stock of kail. Joining hand in hand they go forth to the kail-yard, previously blind-folded, lads, lasses, and children, equally anxious to have their fortunes told as their seniors. Pulling the first stock they meet with, they immediately return to the light to have an examination of its qualities; its being large or little, straight or crooked, is prophetic of the size and shape of its puller's conjugal companion. If any earth adheres to the root, it indicates tocher or fortune; and the taste of the custoc or stem, whether sour or sweet, shows the nature of his disposition.

They go next to the barn-yard, and pull each a stalk of oats, and according to the number of grains upon the stalk the puller will have a corresponding number of children. It may be observed, that it is essential to a female's good fame that her stalk should have the top-grain attached to it.

An individual goes to the barn, opens both its doors, then takes the instrument used in winnowing corn, called a *wecht*, and goes through all the gestures of letting down corn against the wind. This is repeated three several times, and the third time an apparition will pass through the barn, in at the one door and out at the other, having a retinue emblematical of his or her station in life.

A person goes privately to *Tor-na-ha*, or the kiln-pot, throws into it a clew of blue thread, which the person winds into a new clew. Towards the latter end something will hold the thread, on which the person demands, "Who holds?" An answer will be returned by the agent below, by naming the Christian name and sirname of the person's future spouse.

A person steals out unperceived to the peat-stack—sows a handful of hemp-seed, calling out something to the following effect:—

"Hemp-seed, I saw thee,

Hemp-seed, I saw thee,

And he who is my true love,

Come after me and pu' thee."

And, on looking over his shoulder, he sees the apparition of the person invoked in the attitude of pulling the hemp, which had immediately grown at the magic command. Or, if hemp-seed is not at hand, let the person take the floor-besom, which he will ride in the manner of a witch three times round the peat-stack, and the last time the apparition will appear to him.

They go one or more to what is called a *dead and living ford*, or, in other words, a ford which has been crossed by a funeral, and observing profound silence, dip the sleeve of their shirt in it. On returning home they go to bed in sight of a fire, and, lying awake in bed, they will observe an apparition, being an exact similitude of the grand object in question, turn the shirt-sleeve, as if to dry the other side.

An individual goes to a public road, which branches in three several directions, (*i. e.* the junction of three roads,) bearing with him the cutty or three-legged stool, on which the person seats himself just on the eve of twelve o'clock; and, as the hour strikes, he hears proclaimed the names of the several persons who shall die in the parish before the next anniversary. *Nota.*—If the person carries along with him articles of wearing-apparel, and throws an article away on the proclamation of each person's name, it will rescue the person from his impending fate; and it will be wise to retain one article to the last, in case his own name may be called, when he has not the means of redemption at hand.

These and some other out-of-door spells having been tried, the parties return to the dwelling-house to burn the nuts. Burning the nuts is a very popular charm. They name a lad and a lass to each particular nut, as they lay them in the fire, and, accordingly, as they burn quietly, or start from beside one another, so the issue of the courtship will be.

A person takes a candle and goes unattended to a looking-glass—eats an apple before it, combing his or her hair all the while, occasionally holding over the shoulder a table-fork with a piece of the apple upon it, and ultimately the adventurer's conjugal partner will be seen in the glass, in the attitude of taking the proffered piece of apple.

These and some other spells of less note, such as dipping for the apple, groping for the clean dish, which are generally known, and, therefore, need not be particularly described, joined to each individual's relation of the sights which he saw on the present and former occasions, together with the reflections they draw from "narrative old age," bring the well-buttered sowans, or more favoured *Banbrishd* upon the table. The *sonsie* kebbock is roasted at the fire, and fangs cut down from end to end. Brandered bannocks, and every other luxury that can be procured, load the hospitable board. The welcome guests surround it; the silver head is bared with solemn reverence, and the temperate feast, qualified with a few rounds of the *Boghtle dhu*, is as much relished as if it consisted of the most delicious luxuries that crown a monarch's board. But the hours are too happy to remain long;—they flee like a shadow, and call the guests to their respective homes. Each swain and damsel now repose themselves on their pillows, full of those tender emotions which the night's amusements excited, and in their midnight slumbers see those objects whose image they so ardently wished to see in all their comeliness and beauty.

CHRISTMAS.

The children of years to come shall hear the fame of Carthon, when they sit round the burning oak, and the night is spent in songs of old.

OSSIAN.

CHRISTMAS EVE is chiefly spent in preparation for the succeeding days. The housewife is busily engaged in the provision and cooking of dainties. The flailman still chaps in the barn, desirous of providing the necessary store of fodder for the Christmas. The herd-boy's axe resounds on the fir-stock, determined to prepare plenty of light, and the gudeman, and others, are abroad on a not less important errand.

This errand, on which we suppose the gudeman and his assistants employed, is the procuring of *Calluch Nollic*, or *Christmas Old Wife*, an indispensable requisite for this occasion; and it will perhaps puzzle some of our readers to guess the purpose for which the good woman is wanted. If they suppose it is to contribute to the hilarity of the time, or to assist in the festive preparations, the idea is not very erroneous—the old woman does so in a very effectual manner. But the return she meets with, however warm, will not be admired by the reader, when he is told that it consists in being stowed into a cartful of burning peats, with as little ceremony and feeling as an old broom. This usage, so inconsistent with the Highlander's characteristic humanity, she does not, however, regard as a great punishment, for her feelings are as fire-proof as those of a Salamander. Indeed, it is no rare sight, though strange it must be, to see an honest woman, who has undergone the unpleasant process of being Christmas fire to a circle of unfeeling fellows, perhaps oftener than once, heartily spinning at her wheel, and gratifying those, it may be, who had a hand in the unfriendly act, with her marvellous tales. But to avoid a certain imputation which some may be inclined to fix on us, it will be proper to explain our meaning.

The reader will please understand, that this good woman only undergoes this process by representation. Among those valuable discoveries which distinguish former ages, that which gave rise to this custom deserves notice. Some wise-acre, by some lucky chance, discovered, that at this festive season, when the asperity of his character is probably much softened, even relentless death himself can be compromised with on very advantageous terms. By the sacrifice of an old woman, or any other body whom he wished in a better world, and whom, by the following process, he chose to send to it, death was debarred from any farther claim to himself, or his friends, until the return of the next anniversary. He went to the wood this night, fetched home the stump of some withered tree, which he regularly constituted the representative of some person of the description we have mentioned, and whose doom was inevitably fixed by the process, without resort or appeal. Such a simple mode of obtaining security from a foe whom every body fears, could not be supposed to fall into desuetude; and the custom is therefore retained, whatever faith may exist as to its utility, in some parts of the country, even to this day.

But to return to the busy fireside whence we set out, we shall suppose the goodman and the "*carling*" arrived, and the other members of the family now relieved from their eager toil, with the old wife in the centre. The question now is, how the remainder of the night is to be disposed of? The nature of it requires that it should be spent with gaiety; and a game at cards, the clod, or the bag, is generally fixed upon. At the ordinary hour, however, all retire to rest with minds bent on the morrow's gratifications, and the house is soon changed from that scene of bustle and confusion it recently exhibited, to that of peaceful tranquillity, where nothing is heard but the slumbering of the inmates, and the growling bark of the faithful *collie* on the midden-head.

At length the brightening glow of the eastern sky warns the anxious housemaid of the approach of

CHRISTMAS DAY.

She rises full of anxiety at the prospect of her morning labours. The meal, which was steeped in the *sowans-bowie* a fortnight ago, to make the *Prechdachdan sour*, or *sour scones*, is the first object of her attention. The gridiron is put on the fire, and the sour scones are soon followed by hard cakes, soft cakes, buttered cakes, brandered bannocks, and pannich perm. The baking being once over, the sowans pot succeeds the gridiron, full of new sowans, which are to be given to the family, agreeably to custom, this day in their beds. The sowans are boiled into the consistence of molasses, when the *Lagan-le-vrich*, to distinguish it from boiled sowans, is ready. It is then poured into as many bickers as there are individuals to partake of it, and presently served to the whole, old and young. It would suit well the pen of a Burns, or the pencil of a Cruikshank, to paint the scene which follows. The ambrosial food is soon dispatched in aspiring draughts by the family, who soon give evident proofs of the enlivening effects of the *Lagan-le-vrich*. As soon as each dispatches his bicker, he jumps out of bed—the elder branches to examine the ominous signs of the day, and the younger to enter on its amusements. Flocking to the swing, a favourite amusement on this occasion, the youngest of the family gets the first "*shouden*," and the next oldest to him, in regular succession. In order to add the more to the spirit of the exercise, it is a common practice with the person in the *swing*, and the person appointed to swing him, to enter into a very warm and humorous altercation. As the swinged person approaches the swinger, he exclaims, *Ei mi tu chal*, "I'll eat your kail." To this the swinger replies, with a violent shove, *Cha ni u mu chal*, "You shan't eat my kail." These threats and repulses are sometimes carried to such a height as to break down or capsize the threatener, which generally puts an end to the quarrel.

As the day advances, those minor amusements are terminated at the report of the gun, or the rattle of the ball-clubs—the gun inviting the marksman to the "*Kiavanuchd*," or prize-shooting, and the latter to "*Luchd-vouil*," or the ball-combatants—both the principal sports of the day. A description of either of these sports is unnecessary, as nothing new distinguishes them from similar amusements in other places; unless it be a consummate precision in the marksman, and a vigorous intrepidity in the ball-combatants, that cannot perhaps be equalled by the peasantry of any other country.

Tired at length of the active amusements of the field, they exchange them for the substantial entertainments of the table. Groaning under the "*sonsy haggis*," and many other savoury dainties, unseen perhaps for twelve months before, the relish communicated to the company, by the appearance of the festive board, is more easily conceived than described. The dinner once dispatched, the flowing bowl succeeds, and the sparkling glass flies to and fro like a weaver's shuttle. As it continues its rounds, the spirits of the company become the more jovial and happy. Animated by its cheering influence, even old decrepitude no longer feels his habitual pains—the fire of youth is in his eye, as he details to the company the exploits which distinguished him in the days of "*auld langsyne*;" while the young, with hearts inflamed with "*love and glory*," long to mingle in the more lively scenes of mirth, to display their prowess and agility. Leaving the patriarchs to finish those professions of friendship for each other, in which they are so devoutly engaged, the younger part of the company will shape their course to the ball-room, or the card-table, as their individual inclinations suggest; and the remainder of the evening is spent with the greatest pleasure of which human nature is susceptible. Nor will this happy evening terminate the festivities of this occasion. Christmas mid-day awakes all but old age, to a renewal of former hilarity. To age, however, there is no permanent enjoyment ordained in this sublunary state. The transient gleam of happiness which animated his feeble frame has given place, with the cause of it, to a gloom proportionate to his former joys. Headaches, rheumatisms, and other wonted infirmities, are this day returned with more than usual virulence. He wakes only to recline his head on a pillow of sorrow, and to think on the days that are gone.

NEW-YEAR'S EVE.

"A gude New Year I wish thee, Maggy."

BURNS.

THE Highlander's native proneness to festive enjoyments, far from being cloyed by recent series of feasts and diversions, only receives from their speedy recurrence an additional excitement. Anxious by all means to secure this occasion its accustomed share of hilarity, fresh schemes of amusement are studied and promoted with unabated avidity. The peculiar character of the time pre-eminently entitles it to every demonstration of satisfaction which mankind can evince; and it must be no small stimulus to the Highlander's laudable zeal, to see that in this he is imitated by beings whose abilities are far inferior to his own.

We presume it is a circumstance that is very little known in other quarters of the kingdom, that, on this particular occasion, even the *brute* creation (if we may use the expression) have an instinctive knowledge of its auspices. In particular, that admirable object of Highland curiosity, the "*Candlemas Bull*," manifests no small degree of respect for the occasion. This strange and curious *animal*, which has so long escaped the observation of all the *Saxon* naturalists and astronomers that ever lived, has been long since discovered by our Highland philosophers. We say astronomers! because, however strange it may appear, this bull forms an object of speculation connected with their department of science. It must not, however, be inferred from this circumstance, that it is of that celestial species of bulls designated by astronomers to distinguish a particular division of the zodiac; neither is it of that terrestrial species known to naturalists and cattle-dealers—it is of a species distinct from both. Partaking together of the aërial and terrestrial nature and qualities, both the earth and the air are equally its elements. This bull makes an annual excursion, in some latitude or other, about the twilight of this night, no doubt in honour of the occasion. He has, it is said, neither wings nor any other apparent buoyants; but he takes advantage of the course of the wind, on which he glides along in fellowship with the clouds, in a manner that would do credit to the best aeronaut of the day. The particular place of his ascension or descent, which varies with the direction of the wind, cannot be exactly ascertained. Nor can we favour the curious with a minute description of its bodily appearance, since we never had the good fortune to be present when it was seen. All our informants, however, agree in representing it as of a very large size, the colour of a dark cloud, and having all the limbs of a common bull.

As soon as night sets in, it is the signal for the suspension of common employments; and the Highlander's attention is directed to more agreeable and important callings. Associating themselves into bands, the men, with tethers and axes, shape their course towards the juniper bushes, which are as much in request this night as kail is on Hallowe'en. Returning home with Herculean loads, the juniper is arranged around the fire to dry till the morning. Some careful person is also dispatched to the *dead and living ford*, who draws a pitcher of water, observing all the time the most profound silence. Great care must be taken that the vessel containing the water does not touch the ground, otherwise it would lose all its virtues. These and every other necessary peculiar to the occasion being provided, the inmates retire to rest for the night, full of the thoughts of the morrow.

The Highlander's morning cheer this day is far less palatable than that with which he is served so comfortably on Christmas-day. But if it be not so agreeable to his temporal inclinations, it is far more beneficial to his spiritual interests. The *Lagan-le-vrich*, though very good in itself as a substantial dish, will do no more than satisfy for a time the cravings of nature. But the treat of which he partakes this day extends its effects to the good of both soul and body. This treat, if we may so call it, is divided into two courses, which are productive of the following good effects.

The first course, consisting of the *Usque-Cashrichd*, or water from the *dead and living ford*, by its sacred virtues, preserves the Highlander, until the next anniversary, from all those direful calamities proceeding from the agency of all infernal spirits, witchcraft, evil eyes, and the like. And the second course, consisting of the fumes of juniper, not only removes whatever diseases may affect the human frame at the time, but it likewise fortifies the constitution against their future attacks. These courses of medicine are administered in the following manner:—

Light and fire being kindled, and the necessary arrangements having been effected, the high priest of the ceremonies for the day, and his assistants, proceed with the hallowed water to the several beds in the house, and, by means of a large brush, sprinkles upon their occupants a profuse shower of the precious preservative, which, notwithstanding its salutary properties, they sometimes receive with jarring ingratitude.

The first course being thus served, the second is about to be administered, preliminary to which it is necessary to stuff all the crevices and windows in the house, even to the key-hole. This done, piles of juniper are kindled into a conflagration in the different apartments of the house. Rising in fantastic curls, the fumes of the blazing juniper spread along the roof, and gradually condense themselves into an opaque cloud, filling the apartment with an odoriferous fumigation altogether overpowering. Penetrating into the inmost recesses of the patient's system, (for *patients* they may well be called,) it brings on an incessant shower of hiccupping, sneezing, wheezing, and coughing, highly demonstrative of its expectorating qualities. But it not unfrequently happens, that young and thoughtless urchins, not relishing such *physic*, and unmindful of the important benefits they reap from it, diversify the scene by cries of suffocation and the like, which never fail to call forth from the more reflecting part of the family, if able to speak, a very severe reproof. Well knowing, however, that the more intense the "*smuchdan*," the more propitious are its effects, the high priest, with dripping eyes and distorted mouth, continues his operations, regardless of the feelings of his flock, until he considers the dose fully sufficient—upon which he opens the *vent*, and the other crevices, to admit the genial fluid, to recover the spirits of the exhausted patients. He then proceeds to gratify the horses, cattle, and other bestial stock in the town, with the same entertainment in their turn.

Meanwhile, the gudewife gets up, venting the most latent embryo of disease in a copious expectoration; and clapping her hand upon the bottle *dhu*, she administers a renovating cordial to the sufferers around her. The painful ordeal is, therefore, soon forgotten, and nothing is heard but the salutations of the season. All the family now get up, to wash their besmeared faces and prepare themselves for the festivities of the day, and for receiving the visits of their neighbours. These last soon arrive in bodies, venting upon the family broadsides of salutation peculiar to the day. Breakfast being served up, consisting of all the luxuries that can be procured, those of the neighbours not engaged are invited to partake of it; and the day is terminated with balls, drinking, card parties, and other sports too tedious to be mentioned.

FASTEN'S EVE.

"And oft I hear your dearest name

Whispered in my troubled dream."

THE most substantial entertainment peculiar to this night is the matrimonial brose, which is a dish, we believe, well known throughout the country at large. This savoury dish is generally made of the bree of a good fat jigget of beef or mutton, which, being sometimes a good while in *retentum*, renders the addition of salt to the meal unnecessary. Before the bree is put in the bicker or plate, a ring is mixed with the meal, which it will be the aim of every partaker to get. The first bicker being discussed, the ring is put into two other bickers successively; and should any of the candidates for matrimony find the ring more than once, he may rest assured of his marrying before the next anniversary.

The brose, and plenty of other good cheer, being dispatched, the guests betake themselves to another part of the night's entertainment. Soon as the evening circle convenes, the *"Bannich Junit,"* or "sauty bannocks," are resorted to. The component ingredients of those dainties are eggs and meal, and a sufficient quantity of salt, in order to sustain their ancient and appropriate appellation of "sauty." These ingredients, well mixed together, are baked or toasted on the gridiron, and are regarded by old and young as a most delicious treat; and, as may be expected, they have a charm attached to them, which enables the happy Highlander to discover the object of all his spells—his connubial bed-fellow.

A sufficient number of those designed for the palate being prepared, the great or matrimonial bannock is made, of which all the young people in the house partake. Into the ingredients of it there is some particle intermixed, which, in the distribution, will fall to the lot of some happy person, who may be sure, if not already married, to be so before the next anniversary.

Last of all are made the *Bannich Bruader*, or dreaming bannocks, to the ingredients composing which is added a little of that substance which chimney-sweeps call soot, and which contains some charm of which we have not yet come to the knowledge. In baking these last bannocks, the baker must be as mute as a stone—one word would destroy the charm of the whole concern. One is given to each individual, who slips off with it quietly to bed; and, reposing his head on his bannock, he will be gratified by the sight of his beloved in the course of his midnight slumbers.

BELTANE EVE.

"Now the sun's gone out o' sight,

Beet the ingle, snuff the light;

In glens the fairies skip and dance,

And witches wallop o'er to France."

RAMSAY.

BELTANE EVE is a night of considerable importance and of much anxiety to the Highland farmer, as being the grand anniversary review night, on which all the tribes of witches, warlocks, wizards, and fairies, in the kingdom, are to be reviewed by Satan and his chief generals in person, and new candidates admitted into infernal orders. When such a troop, under such a commander, are let loose upon the community, it is natural to suppose that much misery and devastation will follow in their train; and when rewards are only conferred on those most consummate in wickedness, and those most adept in cutting diabolical cantrips, it is natural for every honest man to feel anxious that they may not obtain promotion at his expense. In order, therefore, to be perfectly secure from the machinations of so dangerous a society, every prudent man will resort to those safeguards that will keep them at the staff's end. Messengers are therefore dispatched to the woods for cargoes of the blessed rowan tree, the virtues of which are well known. Being formed into the shape of a cross, by means of a red thread, the virtues of which too are very eminent, those crosses are, with all due solemnity, inserted in the different door-lintels in the town, and protect those premises from the cantrips of the most diabolical witch in the universe. Care should also be taken to insert one of them in the midden, which has at all times been a favourite site of *rendezvous* with the black sisterhood. This cheaply purchased precaution once observed, the people of those countries will now go to bed as unconcernedly, and sleep as soundly, as on any other night.

While those necessary precautions are in preparation, the matron or housekeeper is employed in a not less interesting avocation to the juvenile generation, *i. e.* baking the Beltane bannocks. Next morning the children are presented each with a bannock, with as much joy as an heir to an estate his title-deeds; and having their pockets well lined with cheese and eggs, to render the entertainment still more sumptuous, they hasten to the place of assignation, to meet the little band assembled on the brow of some sloping hill, to reel their bannocks, and learn their future fate. With hearty greetings they meet, and with their knives make the signs of life and death on their bannocks. These signs are a cross, or the sign of life, on the one side; and a cypher, or the sign of death, on the other. This being done, the bannocks are all arranged in a line, and on their edges let down the hill. This process is repeated three times, and if the cross most frequently present itself, the owner will live to celebrate another Beltane day; but if the cypher is oftenest uppermost, he is doomed to die of course. This sure prophecy of short life, however, seldom spoils the appetites of the unfortunate short-livers, who will handle their knives with as little signs of death as their more fortunate companions. Assembling around a rousing fire of collected heath and brushwood, the ill-fated bannocks are soon demolished, amidst the cheering and jollity of the youthful association.

CHRISTENINGS.

"When we sit bowsing at the nappy,

And getting fu' and unco happy,

We think not on the lang Scots miles,

The mosses, waters, slaps, an' stiles."

BURNS.

HAVING travelled over the prominent features which distinguish public annual festivities in the Highlands of Scotland, we shall now briefly direct the reader's attention to those particular occasions which only interest private circles of friends; and of all these it may be said, that the birth and christening of a child forms one of the most pleasant and important. The fond parent, filled with those visionary hopes and expectations which the imagination is so apt to conceive as the portion of those objects most dear to us, fancies he beholds in his new offspring the future hero or statesman, whose fragile hand may be destined to wield the sword of a general or the pen of a statesman. Such is the impression of the Highland parent in particular—an impression in which he is perhaps confirmed by superior authority. The great utility and comfort derived from having the assistance of those wise people, whose experience and judgment enable them to discover those great destinies in an infant, is abundantly apparent; and of this capacity most of the Highland matrons are possessed. It is no doubt this weighty consideration that induces every honest woman to have her own junto of matron counsellors, whose presence is as indispensable on the occasion of an accouchement as that of the *accoucheur*. If the offspring is a son, it is likely those sage physiognomists will already trace in his infantile lineaments clear signs of that future greatness which he is destined some happy day to display, as well as the striking resemblance he bears to his father and mother. The greatness of such a *blessing* as this they never fail to impress upon the overjoyed father, (though, by the bye, he may have had too many of these blessings before,) who is thus induced cheerfully to devote more of his little property than he can well afford, to give the occasion its deserved *eclat*. Filled with pleasure, elated with hope, Highland hospitality has no bounds—a score of lives are sacrificed at the shrine of festivity, and all the neighbours and kinsmen invited to the christening. The day arrived, the little great man destined to grace some name is arrayed in his robes of state, and confided to the care of the happy sponsors, who, (should the parson not attend the feast,) together with the company present, will proceed with him to the parsonage, to receive the ordinance of baptism. On their return, the guests assembled will pledge the health of their host and the *Benheen*, or the sick wife, in overflowing bumpers—not forgetting young Donald, who, "*may he thrive*," every body praises for a fine child.

The seating and tables being next sorted in some snug place, the feast commences with a course of savoury soup, which is pronounced good by all. A succeeding course of broth is still better; and a third still better than the second. Mutton and beef follow, each good in its kind. Plenty of fowls, equally delicious, are next ushered in, calling forth the unqualified praise of the guests, who, upon the whole, pronounce the banquet the most luxurious which they have seen for a long time before. The dessert once dispatched, the flowing bowl succeeds, and the rafters are made again to resound to the healths of the young hero and his parents. A long catalogue of those toasts and sentiments most congenial to the feelings of the company are next drank with the greatest glee; and bowl after bowl is speedily drained "to *friendship's growth*," the effects of which bespeak themselves in the aspect of the company.

Enveloped in a cloud of tobacco-smoke, in one corner a hamlet politician is retailing to his half-attentive neighbour the various news of the day. Another guest is as warmly engaged in the praise of his wife, his horses, or his cattle; and another is eagerly soliciting attention to his improved mode of ploughing his ground, sowing his turnips, and planting his potatoes. At length, when the house begins to revolve, each thinks it time to withdraw. The officious midwife then comes to the door, full of kind inquiries, if each has got his own plaid, bonnet, and staff; and being rewarded for her attention by the customary *douceur*, she wishes them all a good night and a pleasant journey.

WEDDINGS.

"Was ne'er in Scotland heard or seen

Sic dancing and deray;

Nouther at Falkland on the green,

Nor Peebles at the play."

KING JAMES I.

INTERESTING as a christening undoubtedly is to the parents of the child, it is, neither in a public nor private sense, so happy an occasion as that which we are about to describe. If there is any thing under the sun in which true happiness really consists, we are told it is in the consummation of a marriage, where the parties, uninfluenced by sordid motives, are entirely brought together by the magnetic power of love. Of such a description the Highland marriages are in general. The lower classes being pretty equal in their circumstances, policy and interest have less influence in their marriages than is the case with any other rank of people; and consequently the parties are left more to the unbiassed dictates of their own voluntary choice.

When a couple of young lovers propose to get married, the nearest relations of both parties meet to take the case into consideration; and, in general, it is no difficult matter for the lovers and their advocates to get a decision consonant to their inclinations. This is called the booking ("*leuruch*") or contract, which is very often ratified by no other covenant than a few bottles of whisky. If the parties come to an understanding, the lovers are immediately declared bride and bridegroom; and some Tuesday or Thursday in the growth of the moon is fixed upon for the celebration of the nuptials. Meanwhile, to sustain the dignity of the bridal pair, from motives of policy as well as of state, they select from their kinsmen two trustworthy persons each, who are delegated to the other—the male to protect the party from being stolen, (a practice once common, and not yet extinct,) and the female to act as maid of honour and lady of the bedchamber on the bridal occasion.

A few days prior to the bridal day, the parties, with their attendants, perambulate the country, inviting the guests, on which occasion they meet with marked attention from old and young. The invitations are all delivered to the parties *propria persona* at their firesides; and if the wedding is to be a cheap one, a small present is sometimes offered to the bride, and accepted of.

On the morning of the wedding-day, some lady, who is above the ordinary level, and who has been constituted mistress of the ceremonies for the day, arrives to deck the bride in her splendid habiliments. She is received by the clean white bride, previously prepared for her by a ducking in the cold bath; and, retiring to the wardrobe chamber, she is speedily metamorphosed from a "sonsy country lassie" into a downright lady—at least, if muslins and ribbons are all that is requisite to confer this distinction, she is entitled to it. The bridegroom, too, at his apartments, has his own decorators, who deck him out most splendidly with marriage favours and other ornaments suitable to the occasion.

Meanwhile, repeated vollies of musketry summon the guests to the wedding. Mounted on his palfry, each "crony" shapes his course to the house to which he was invited; while droves of youngsters flock along the road, whose hearts at every shot are bounding with joy. On their arrival, they are ushered into the breakfasting apartment, to partake of the forenoon's entertainment, consisting of good milk porridge and cream, on which they fare very sumptuously. After this mid-day repast, they are led to the ball-room, or dancing apartment, to share in its enjoyment. Here the bride or bridegroom is seated at the upper end of the ball-room, and receives the company, as they successively arrive, with great pomp and ceremony; and the dancing and mirth is prolonged for some hours.

At the time appointed, the bridegroom selects a party of young men, who are dispatched to summon the bride and her party to the marriage ceremony. Their approach is announced by showers of musketry opened upon them by some of the bride's men, and returned, most of the guests being furnished with pistols. The bride's party accordingly prepare themselves for the procession. The bride is mounted upon some *canny* charger behind an expert rider; drams go round to her health and prosperity; and, the company being all in readiness, she leaves her native residence for another, amidst the cheers and *feu-de-joie* of the assembly. Marching to the sound of the inspiring bagpipes, and the discharge of fire-arms, the bride's party proceed to the place appointed for the marriage. The bridegroom's party follow at some little distance; and both arrived at the appointed place of rendezvous, the bridegroom's party stand in the rear till the bride's party enter the meeting-house, agreeably to the rules of precedence, which on this occasion are decidedly in favour of the bride in all the proceedings of the day.

Soon as the hymeneal knot is tied, the candidates for the honour of wonning the kail, as they call it, drive off *pell mell* for the bridegroom's house, horsemen and footmen promiscuously. Both parties, now mingled together, proceed with multitudinous joviality towards the bridegroom's, the scene of the future festivities of the night. A volley of fire-arms announces their arrival; and the company assembled at the door, to welcome the bride, assail her with a basket of the bridal bread and cheese, the properties of which are well known. The bridal pair are then seated at the upper end of the banquet, and the guests are arrayed, according to their quality, around the far-extended tables, formed of doors, chests, and cart bottoms, sustained by sturdy supporters of wood or stone; and wooden beams, and deals for chairs, in common form. The more plebeian part of the guests, freely disposed of in the stables or byres, make themselves very comfortable with their cheer.

Shortly the waiters come round the circle, presenting each with a spoon, which he must carefully return when done with it. The spoon is followed with the hardly-contested kail. After this, a remove of savoury broth is presently brought in; of which all having partaken, the still more delicious "*hotch-potch*" succeeds. Then follow fowl of every feather, and every beast and creeping thing—

"Hind and fore spalls of a sheep

Drew whittles frae ilk sheath;

Wi' gravie a' their beards did creep,

They kempit wi' their teeth."

The dinner being over, the "shemit reel" is the next object of attention. All the company assemble on the lawn with flambeaux, and form into a circle. The bridal pair and their retinue then dance a *sixsome reel*, each putting a piece of silver into the musician's hand. Those desirous may then succeed, and dance with the bride and the two maids of honour, and are gratified at the commencement and termination of each reel by the usual salutes.

In the meantime, the stewards of the feast having removed the temporary erections from the dancing apartments, the shemit reel being over, the guests re-occupy their seats in the original order, and dancing and mirth is again resumed. Tartan plaids, spreading in every corner, invite the fair to take shelter in those most congenial to their inclinations. The jovial smiling bowl, now reeking in a corner, allures to its side its votaries—the circling glass adds additional stimulus to the riotous spirit of the company. In short, pleasure presents herself for courtship in all her luring forms.

As the night advances, the company grows still more happy. The numerous ills of the human lot, which at other times so much afflict them, now cause them no concern; on the contrary, they are entirely full of its pleasures.

Hence, all the corners of the house, instead of declamations against the infirmities of age, or the badness of the times, are full of the happiest communications. Opportunities long sought for declaring secret friendship have now occurred, and the warmth with which they are expressed forcibly bespeak their fervency. Two patriarchs "had long indulged the hope of seeing an honourable alliance betwixt *their* families. Both honest and respectable, the union of their children would be a highly suitable match; and should such a desirable event ever occur, there was a black stocking in secret, which would spew on the occasion of the wedding." In another, you may see two hearty grey-beards, whose locked hands and contacting noddles show the closeness of their friendship, relating to each other, with much complacency, those tales of "*auld langsyne*" in which they themselves acted so prominent a part. In another corner, the fond lover, with his dearly beloved locked in his affectionate embrace, melting her heart with his wooing strains; and in another, the vocal choir, whose throats of steel vociferate their harmonious ditties on the gratified ears of the company; while, on the top of a bed, or at the back of the door, the juvenile part of the guests, assembled in tumultuous rabble, will also join their voices in the general uproar.

On the floor the dancers are beyond compare. Fixed with emulation who shall *win the dance*, every nerve and muscle is put in active exercise. The lads are gaining greater agility every successive reel; while, in the language of the poet,

"The lasses bab'd about the reel,

Gart a' their hurdies wallop,

And swat like ponies when they speel

Up braes, or when they gallop."

This scene lasts for some hours, until the presence of day warns the bride to prepare for the bedding. Wishing, if possible, to elude the public gaze, she attempts to steal away privately, when, observed by some vigilant eye, her departure is announced, and all push to the bridal chamber.

The door is instantly forced open, and the devoted bride, divested of all her braws, and stripped nearly to the state of nature, is placed in bed in presence of the whole company. Her left stocking is then flung, and falls upon some individual, whose turn to the hymeneal altar will be the next. The bridegroom, next led in, is as rapidly demolished, and cosily stowed along-side of his darling. A bottle and glass being then handed to the bridegroom, he rewards the friendliness of those who come forward to offer their congratulations, with a flowing bumper. When the numerous levée have severally paid their court, they retire, and leave the young couple to repose.

On returning to the grand scene of festivity, we shall find that the aspect of the company there has suffered no small alteration during our absence. Overpowered by the peculiar influence of the ardent friendship which fills the elder branches of the company, those boisterous expressions of esteem which recently occupied them so much, have declined into the calmest complacency. Overcome by the most unspeakable sensations, the tongue, which was lately so voluble, has totally failed. Those legs, which but a few hours ago displayed the greatest agility, have now refused their office; and the whole machine is become perfectly unwieldy and unmanageable:

"In their mawes there was na mank;

Upon the firms some snor'd;

Ithers frae aff the bunkers sank,

Wi' een like collops scor'd."

Seated by the victorious bowl, the *Far Cuil* is still engaged in his musical vocation. With bow alternately above and below the strings, he is earnestly employed at *Tullochgorum*, while cries for the same spring, proceeding from the dancers on the floor, incessantly ring on his ears. Insensible to time or measure, some of the young people still wallop on the floor, and unabated clamour reigns throughout the house.

Meanwhile, all the avenues leading from the town are thronged with retiring guests *"careering"* on their way home; and the company is ultimately reduced to the immediate friends and relations of the young couple, who wait to offer their morning congratulations. When the bridal pair are supposed to have reposed themselves sufficiently long, they are warned to get up, to prepare for the breakfast and the morning levée. On entering the grand breakfasting parlour, the whole concourse of friends receive them with showers of compliments and congratulations, accompanied by such gifts as may be convenient; and yesterday's scene of festivity is again renewed, and prolonged for the day.

WAKES.

"But turn to yonder cloister'd gloom,

Where pallid Sorrow leads the way,

To muse upon some hallow'd tomb,

Where Friendship's dearest relics lie."

W. S.

SHORT and unstable are the joys of man!—How often does it happen that such ardent scenes of pleasure as we have been just endeavouring to describe are but like the gleam which precedes the storm—a prelude to direful woe! Oft has the tender parent or loving child, who but yesterday animated such a scene of festivity, to-day exhibited the most desponding spectacle which human nature can witness. Those eyes, which then sparkled at the *pibroch's* harmonious sounds, are now sealed for ever; and his relations and friends are involved in grief more vehement than their former joys.

Prone to partake in his neighbour's joys, the Highlander, on such occasions as this, is equally ready to share in his sorrows, and will not grudge to contribute his exertions, by night as well as by day, to add to his comfort or consolation. On the last offices of friendship being performed, the body is laid on a bed in that apartment of the house most commodious and suitable for the company; and the neighbours immediately collect in bands, to watch over the remains of departed friendship. During the silent hours of midnight, the solemnity of the occasion is heightened by the sound of sacred praise, and reading of the blessed Gospel. Such are now the laudable employments which have assumed the place of that revelry which formerly disgraced the Highland wakes, when immoderate drinking, dancing, wanton levity, and profane amusements, were the prominent features of such an assembly. It is true, the moderate use of liquor and singing of songs are still tolerated, but excess on these occasions is now unknown. On the departure of every group, one of the friends in attendance conducts them to the melancholy bier, when each generally testifies the ardour of his friendship by shaking the hand, which now cannot feel his proffered kindness, and retires full of those solemn reflections which the scene is calculated to produce.

FUNERALS.

"In some fond breast still lives the face,

Its wonted smile, the darling form,

Which awful death cannot efface,

However much it may deform."

W. S.

ON the third day after the defunct's decease, if the person occupied no station above the ordinary level, the body will be led to its destined abode. This sorrowful day is early distinguished by melancholy arrangements. Verbal warnings having been previously circulated to the male inhabitants of the district, large and timeous preparations are necessary for their accommodation and entertainment. While the seating of the apartments destined to receive the company occupies the men, the arrangement of the entertainment occupies no less the attention of the women. In the meanwhile, the relations and family of the deceased attire themselves in the best mournings their circumstances can afford, and prepare themselves for going through the duties of the day with all possible fortitude and decency. The arrival of the wooden house of death, and the deposition of its inhabitant, early call forth many a sigh and tear at the parting which is about to take place. But the closing of the coffin is deferred till the eve of removal.

About twelve o'clock, the company, or, to speak more properly, the guests, successively arrive in scattered groups, dressed in all the variegated colours of the rainbow; and are received by some near connection of the deceased, who conducts them to the place appointed for their station.

With becoming gravity they take their seats, condoling very feelingly with the present friends on their lamentable loss, and carry on for a while a conversation very suitable to the business which brought them together. They are each served, on their arrival, with what is called a dram of "*dry whisky*," and some fit person is appointed to keep the glass in active circulation. To him is also delegated a discretionary power of imposing extra penalties on late comers, who must compensate for their absence by drinking a double quantity on their arrival.

Thus, all equally well plied with the enlivening glass, the solemn aspect of the company is soon changed into a mixture of sorrow and joy. The moralist, who so recently uttered such sage reflections upon the shortness of life and its uncertainty, is transformed by some secret influence into the sprightly wit, whose humorous jokes and repartees continually agitate the risible powers of his audience. In short, the house of mourning is rapidly changing into a house of mirth; and such would be the opinion of any stranger who might visit the scene.

As soon as he approaches the door of the *meeting-house*, his ears are assailed with a confusion of sounds, which conveys to him the idea of entering a house full of bees. Seated in double rows, extending from one end of the house to the other, he finds it literally crammed, not with bees, but Highlandmen of every age and condition. In each end of the house he sees overflowing bowls, and walking to and fro, a host of waiters, bearing the full and empty glasses of the company, followed by others with bread and cheese, which are liberally distributed amongst the guests. Being seated in the place befitting his rank or station, if curiosity leads him to a closer examination of the complexion of his company, he will not be a little amused at the diversity of feelings and conversation distinguishing the individuals composing it. If the visitor or stranger whom we have supposed is of a serious cast of mind, and if he addresses himself to his elbow neighbour on the solemn character of the occasion, and laments the pitiful state of the family that may be thus deprived of their parent or provider— perhaps, if he listens for a moment with counterfeited seriousness, the sprightly sally of a rustic wit rings upon his ear, and a horse-laugh immediately shows the spectator he has no great relish for his subject. If, again, he addresses himself to one of a less jovial temperament, who has not yet been so much affected by the general *infection* upon the same subject, he will perhaps acknowledge the justness of his observations with a significant shake of the head, declaring at the same time the poignancy of his sorrow for the deceased, who, "new peace to him, was the best of souls." But, at the same time, and in the same breath, he will make a digression to the alarming depreciation of agricultural produce, and the consequent inevitable ruin of poor farmers, if they do not immediately get a reduction of the one-half of their rents; and the concern he evinces for both matters makes it difficult to determine which loss he considers the greater calamity. Listening to the various topics of conversation discussed by the company in general, he will find *seriousness* form no part of it. Having already sufficiently moralized on the *evils* of life, they are now resolved to confine themselves entirely to its *goods*. Death, low prices, and high rents, have now given place to balls, feasts, and diversions. One group is warmly engaged in scheming a "*dry or wet ball*;" another group is warmly expatiating upon the good signs of the year, corroborated as they are by the "*annual prognostic*;" and others are as warmly engaged in recriminating each other for their notorious gallantries, and the like; while a good spring, a good harvest, and ready sale to sheep and cattle, are drunk by all with the greatest enthusiasm. All are become suddenly acquainted with the proverb, "A pound of care will not pay an ounce of debt;" and therefore they are determined to spend life in friendship and good hopes. In obedience to this wholesome resolution, each crony, as he gives his neighbour the hand, will also give him the pipe or the "sneeshan mill," and would be very sorry to see him ill-used in a "*pley*," or any such cause, without rendering him a helping hand.

As the drinking continues, the company become still more noisy. Repetitions of toasts, the vacant laugh, and incoherent exclamation, mingled with a few little oaths, are what perpetually burst upon the ear; and the sequel of such unhallowed carousals exhibit but too frequently a scene of the most improper levity.

Far different, however, are the feelings and conduct of those mournful individuals who occupy another apartment, where the affectionate widow or fatherless orphans are now assembled, to take the last and long farewell of the relics of love. In deep dismay, behold the sorrowing group bending over the dear remains, absorbed in frantic woe, bathing with their tears unfeeling death, insensible to all their sorrows.

When the weeping relatives have severally bade the corpse the last adieu, by imparting the farewell kiss to the cold and pallid lip of death, (which, nevertheless, is perhaps the sweetest we ever impart,) the dearest form is for ever concealed from their view.

"Long on the lip the kiss will dwell,

And on the ear the mournful sigh,

Which seal'd the last and fond farewell,

And forg'd a bond time can't untie."

The necessary arrangements being effected, the coffin is brought forth, surrounded by the bereaved friends, and bound on the *hanspecks* on some convenient supports at the door; and when time will no longer permit the guests to indulge in their hilarity, an unwelcome summons invites them to their duty. Issuing forth tumultuously, they surround their charge; and all the riders being provided with their horses, the signal for setting off is given. The female relations, according to the custom of some countries, get the first lift; and the supports on which the body was bound being carefully overturned, for some reason best known to the wise men of the day, the multitudinous procession takes the road.

At this moment a scene presents itself to the cool spectator, wholly without a parallel. The various habiliments of the company—riders and pedestrians mingled together—the sound of the horses—and the united clamour of the multitude—are altogether striking. At one time, the expressions of mirth predominate; while, at others, the heart-rending lamentations of the female relations of the defunct prevail, and in their turn vibrate upon the ear. The women, at length unwillingly disentangled from the body, return home with mournful wailing, and the procession continues its course to its destination. Too many of the company are sometimes more intent upon their own pleasures than mindful of their business, roving about in scattered parties; while others exhibit, in their attention, a pattern of correctness and decorum; and, warmly enumerating the good qualities of the deceased, descant on the happy change he has made—at the same time walking with a careful step, lest an unfortunate fall beneath the body should doom themselves to share his enviable lot.

At length, arrived at the mansions of the dead, the body is lowered into its drear abode, amidst the sorrowing of some and the insensibility of others. The slate planted on the grave terminates its earthly career, and consigns it for ever to the land of forgetfulness.

"Yet, though consign'd to death's dark shade,

And ever hid from mortal view,

Still constant Love, by Fancy led,

The dreary scene will oft review."

The End.

J. S. WITHERDEN, Lithographic and Letterpress Printer,
Clifford's Inn Passage, Fleet Street.

FOOTNOTES:

Nothing can appear more surprising to the refined reader, than that any human being, possessing the rational faculties of human nature, could for a moment entertain a notion so preposterous as that a ghost, which conveys the idea of an immortal spirit, could be killed, or rather annihilated, by an arrow, dirk, or sixpence. It was, however, the opinion of the darker ages, that such an exploit as killing a ghost was perfectly practicable. A spirit was supposed to be material in its nature, quite susceptible of mortal pain, and liable to death or annihilation from the weapons of man. Such an opinion is repeatedly expressed in several passages of the Poems of Ossian, and in the doctrine of the *Seanachy*, down to the present day.

John-o'-Groat's House, Caithness.

We are informed that there is a woman still living in the parish of Abernethy, on whom this experiment was tried. She was found one night, rather unaccountably, as it appeared to her wise parents, on the outside of a window. No doubt, therefore, remained, but that she had been stolen by the fairies, and a stock left as her substitute. It was, therefore, unanimously resolved to carry the stock to the junction of the shires of Inverness, Moray, and Banff, where the poor child was left for a night to enjoy the pleasures of solitude. Being well rolled up in a comfortable blanket, she sustained no material injury from this monstrous exposure, and, accordingly, the result proved highly satisfactory to her enlightened guardians.

Mine is yours, and yours is mine.

The goats are supposed to be upon a very good understanding with the fairies, and possessed of more cunning and knowledge than their appearance bespeaks.

Witchcraft.

A Witch.

The present Lord Murray is supposed to have been the gentleman who discovered to Mr. Willox this convenient piece of information regarding the original nature and use of the *stone*.

North.

Since the first publication of this book, the renowned Mr. Mac Grigor Willox has been laid with his fathers, leaving the stone and bridle to his son and daughter, as heirlooms for the benefit of posterity. The goodman died full of years, if not full of any thing else which is coveted by the people of this world. But by his death it is believed that the spell which so long bound the northern community to his stone and bridle has been broken; and it is thought that those precious relics, which were scarcely "honestly come by," may be returned to the kelpie and the mermaid, their original owners, should they or their representatives be disposed to claim restitution of them.

The highly curious and interesting collection of Criminal Trials, recently published by Robert Pitcairn, Esq., affords ample particulars of the *modus operandi* by which the workers of Satan in human shape accomplished their nefarious ends. The reader is particularly referred to the cases of those witches of quality, Lady Glammis and Lady Munro of Fowlis, and to the assistant hags of the latter, consisting of Laskie Loncart, Christy Ross, and others, all highly deserving of *record*. But Isobel Gowdie, the head witch of Auldearn, who, on her own confession, was condemned to be "worried and burned at a stake" in 1662, is the standard authority to refer to on these subjects. It appears that in those days Auldearn, near Nairn, now the locality of a virtuous community, was the great nursery that supplied Satan with *cadets* for his "Black Watch;" for so numerous were the members of the craft at that place, according to Isobel Gowdie, that on occasions of public inspection by the sovereign of the order, they were counted or told off in *squads* or "*covines*" (as Isobel called them), to each of which were appointed two *adjutants* or *drill-sergeants*, the brigade-major being a "*well-favoured*" wench of the name of "*Nannie*," who occupied the seat of honour at Satan's *carousals*. On such occasions of assembly, they dug up graves, possessed themselves of unchristened infants, using their joints and members in their incantations. They metamorphosed themselves into the forms of crows, cats, hares, &c., and played all manners of cantrips on live stock and farm produce. But it not unfrequently happened that those *amusements* turned out but indifferent *sport* to some of the *probationers* concerned,—several worthies, and Isobel Gowdie among the rest, having had unwittingly become the subjects of the *chase*, at the feet and mouths of the greyhounds of the day, who have "no respect of persons," or the characters in which they enacted their parts. And it would also appear that the cadets in this Royal Military College formed any thing but an harmonious society—the Master General, and his *Sappers* and *Miners*, often quarrelling about very minor matters, such as titles of distinction; in the course of which the *master* often received many *black names*, and the apprentices many *stripes*. But it would appear that "one Margaret Wilson in Auldearn" was nearly match for him; for Isobel Gowdie declares she used to "*bell the cat*" with him stoutly; "defending herself finely" from the *wool-cards* and such other sharp instruments of punishment as he made use of on those occasions. "It was no doubt one of those ancient *covines* that encountered Macbeth (not far from the College) on his way to Forres."

But since the days of Isobel Gowdie, Maggy Wilson, Bessy Hay, and Co, the *union* has been repealed, without the aid of any great agitator; for ever since their day, the people in this parish have died a natural death. But it is still mooted, "*sotto voce*," that there are still some roots of the old tree scattered over neighbouring territories not far from the capital of the Highlands, who have been allowed to live quite as long as they deserved. And one Isabella Hay, probably a descendant of her namesake of Auldearn, has for many years levied *blackmail* on the inhabitants of Inverness, until having, by her imps, in autumn 1839, laid her enchantments on the goods and chattels of some people in Inverness (the author among the number), she was sentenced in September, 1839, by the Circuit Court of Justiciary—not to the *stake*, but to a punishment which, however, has served to put an end to her sorceries.

Among recent discoveries of the author as charms, or rather counter-charms against witchcraft, it deserves to be noticed, that if a knot tied against the sun be made on the tail of a quadruped, it is secure against the spells of necromancy. It is, or had been till recently, also a common practice to put a portion of the medicinal herb or plant called "*saffron*" under the churn while the process of churning the cream is undergoing, which will prevent the *craft* from taking the substance by means of their magical *rope*, by the operations of which they were wont to extract from a piece of wood in their own dwellings the soul and substance of what might belong to parties afar off, and who, without such precaution, might churn away till doomsday without the appearance of the yellow treasure. And moistening the mouth of a calf with the extract of the said vegetable, and setting it to suck a cow whose milk might go to the said *rope*, will instantly restore it to the proper owner.

It need scarcely be added, in conclusion, that *scoring* a witch crosswise on the forehead, or above her breath, divests her of all supernatural power. But the laws are now so strong, even at John-o'-Groat's house, that the processes of trial by *swimming* and *scoring* cannot now be resorted to, except in *extreme* cases where the *subjects* have not the benefit of *law* or *clergy*. On a very recent occasion, however, in Ross-shire, a worthy fisher, whose nets suffered no small prejudice from the machinations of a neighbour, but no friend, performed on her, much against her consent, the operation of *scoring* on the forehead, for which the sheriff of Ross, in August 1845, sentenced him to undergo a short imprisonment in the gaol of Tain.

Switched cream.

The game called "*Clodhan*," or Clod, is a favourite amusement with the youth in the Highlands. One of the company goes round the circle with a clod, or some other article, putting his hand into each person's lap or hand,

and leaves the clod with one of the number. The whole circle are then desired to guess the person who possesses the clod, (he guessing like the rest to prevent suspicion,) when all those who err are subjected to a small penalty, which shall be afterwards determined by an appointed judge; and in the meantime, he must deliver some pledge to enforce his compliance with the arbiter's decision. When a sufficient number of pledges are obtained, judgment is pronounced against their owners, who must redeem them, by doing various little penances, some of which are sufficiently ludicrous.

The bag is another popular juvenile amusement. One pops his head into a bag, holding his hand spread on his back, and the palm uppermost. One of the company, in rotation, strikes his hand, not unfrequently with all his might, upon that of the person in the bag, who is desired to guess who struck him last. If his guessing proves correct, the last striker then puts his head in the bag in his turn.

Half-boiled sowans.

"A black Christmas makes a fat kirk-yard." A windy Christmas and a calm Candlemas, or new year, are signs of a good year.

The term *Candlemas* is applied to the *New Year* in the Highlands. The origin of the term arose from some old religious ceremonies performed on this occasion by candle-light.

We are totally unable to account for the origin of this strange piece of superstition. It is unnecessary to remark, that the object of this delusion is nothing but a passing cloud, which the perverted imagination of the original Highlander shapes into the form of a bull. There is something very ominous as to the art or direction in which the bull rises or falls—we believe it to be prognostic of its being a good or bad year.

It is believed that this extraordinary entertainment is now administered in no part of the Highlands, except in Strathdown and its immediate neighbourhood. In that district, however, the inhabitants generally attend to it, merely, it is believed, from the influence of inveterate custom, and the author in his day had his share of the antidote, though it is doubtful whether those rites are now observed in his native district.

The literal expressions used in the salutation applicable to this day in the Gaelic language the writer could never perfectly comprehend. The literal translation of the words are, (*Mu nasc choil orst,*) "My Candlemas bond upon you." The real meaning of the words, however, is, "You owe me a New-Year's gift;" and it is a point of great emulation who will salute the other first—the one who does so being considered entitled to a gift from the person so saluted.

Beltane is derived from two Gaelic words conjoined: "*Paletein*," signifying Pale's fire, and not *Baal's fire*, as some suppose. The strange relic of Pagan idolatry which gave rise to this feast was no doubt introduced into these countries, like many others of our more prominent superstitions, by the Druids. Pales (of whom we read in the heathenish mythologies) was the goddess of shepherds, and protectress of flocks. Her feast was always celebrated in the month of April, on which occasion no victim was killed, and nothing was offered but the fruits of the earth. The shepherds purified their flocks with the smoke of sulphur, juniper, boxwood, rosemary, &c. They then made a large fire, round which they danced, and offered to the goddess milk, cheese, eggs, &c., holding their faces towards the east, and uttering ejaculations peculiar to the occasion. Those interesting relics of the religious opinions of our ancestors, until of late, remained pretty entire in some parts of the Highlands. But they have now, however, declined into those childish ceremonies above described.

Mr. Pennant, in his Tour, vol. i. p. 111, notices the ceremony of the Bolteen or Beltane—the cakes baken with scrupulous attention to rites and forms, and dedicated to birds of prey, &c., or the being whose agents they were, to propitiate them to spare the lives of themselves and flocks. Within the last twenty or thirty years these observances have almost wholly disappeared. But the author himself is old enough to have reeled his bannock, and dived, by the foregoing spells, into the secrets of futurity.

Let not the Highland reader be led to view this description of a Highland funeral as casting any reflection on his moral or religious character. Whatever ill-timed levity he may manifest on such an occasion, the blame must be ascribed, not to him, but to that *evil spirit*, the usquebaugh, the real cause of it. We cannot, however, help regretting, that either the ill-judged hospitality of the entertainer, or his own social habits, should expose him on this particular occasion to the unruly influence of his demoralising countryman; and we are glad to add, that of late years much improvement has been effected in the conduct of Highland funerals—sobriety and decorum being much more the order of the day.

A fall sustained by a person, while supporting the body, is ominous of the person's speedy death. It may also be remarked, that it is considered very imprudent to look at a passing funeral from the door of a house, or from the window having a *stone lintel*.

9 789361 473265